Citizen Journalism and Public Sphere: Unveiling the Power of the People's Voice

AMAL JITH RAVEENDRAN

Copyright © <2025> <Amal Jith Raveendran>

All Rights Reserved.

This book has been self-published with all reasonable efforts taken to make the material error-free by the author. No part of this book shall be used, reproduced in any manner whatsoever without written permission from the author, except in the case of brief quotations embodied in critical articles and reviews.

The Author of this book is solely responsible and liable for its content including but not limited to the views, representations, descriptions, statements, information, opinions and references. The Content of this book shall not constitute or be construed or deemed to reflect the opinion or expression of the Publisher or Editor. Neither the Publisher nor Editor endorse or approve the Content of this book or guarantee the reliability, accuracy or completeness of the Content published herein and do not make any representations or warranties of any kind, express or implied, including but not limited to the implied warranties of merchantability, fitness for a particular purpose. The Publisher and Editor shall not be liable whatsoever for any errors, omissions, whether such errors or omissions result from negligence, accident, or any other cause or claims for loss or damages of any kind, including without limitation, indirect or consequential loss or damage arising out of use, inability to use, or about the reliability, accuracy or sufficiency of the information contained in this book.

www.notionpress.com

Contents

About the Author

Amal Jith Raveendran, hailing from Calicut, Kerala, is an alumnus of the Department of Electronic Media and Mass Communication at Pondicherry Central University. He currently serves as an Assistant Professor in the Department of Visual Communication at Kalasalingam University, Madurai, Tamil Nadu.

He has authored several books, including:

- Acting Gender: Gender Discourses in Malayalam Cinema
- Once Upon a Time in Mollywood: A Brief History of Malayalam Cinema
- Panan Kavalayile Manushyar (in Malayalam)

A dedicated educator and researcher, Amal focuses on cinema, media, and social change, contributing significantly to the discourse on these subjects.

Email: amaljithravi245@gmail.com

Foreword

In an era of information explosion, journalists are anointed with the responsibility of verifying facts before publishing information. But who will upheave the roof, when the fourth pillar is biased, promotes hate and fails to question those in authority? Enter, 'The fifth pillar'.

I am very much delighted to acknowledge that my friend, Mr. Amal Jith Raveendran, has aptly termed citizen journalism as the fifth estate. The designation of the press as the fourth estate dates back to the aftermath of the French Revolution. Amal's masterpiece emerges in an era, where, revolution stands as a very distant possibility and even solitary dissent against the authority is swiftly suppressed using power. His book taps into a widely recognized yet underexplored domain, thoroughly examining the concept of citizen journalism, or the so-called 'fifth estate.'

This book serves as a comprehensive resource on all aspects of citizen journalism. Having the privilege of knowing the author personally, I can attest to his deep empathy for the oppressed and the voiceless. As you navigate through the pages, you embark on a journey with Amal, who implores the reader to reject silence and to speak out boldly.

The rise of citizen journalism is very prevalent now with the surge in internet and gadgets. However, in the Indian context citizen journalism played a crucial role during the Kashmir conflict when the government systematically shut down the internet. Several issues such as the Hathras Rape Case, Military dominance in North-East, the Manipur violence, Natural calamity in Uttarakhand and Kerala were brought to light with the help of citizen journalism.

How can we talk about this topic without mentioning the pandemic? At a time when journalists and camera persons were diagnosed with covid-19 and some even losing their lives, the pictures and videos from the public helped gather support. People suffering without oxygen, lack of beds, health staff apathy, and so on were brought to the spotlight.

This said, we must never forget that citizen journalism is a beast. A beast which must be trained and put on leash with regular monitoring. When tamed, it can help root out injustice and give voice to the voiceless. But the same, when unchecked can affect lives quite directly and taint the freedom it has.

We have seen first-hand how old videos which are repurposed can be used in instigating hatred. Perfect example would be an old video which was circulated claiming that Muslims spread the virus purposefully. This resulted in several lynchings and deaths across the country and years later the Supreme Court ruled out that the video was misinformation. If Goebbels were alive, he would have exploited this arena to its full extent. Not just because he was an evil propagandist, but citizen journalism, like mentioned before, is a beast of destruction in the wrong hands.

Concerns about citizen journalism will forever remain, until a robust government and technological mechanism is used to prevent false information. According to NCRB data, not more than 1000 cases are registered until 2022. While actively looking out to voice the injustice and bias in this country, we also need to keep an eye out for videos surfacing on social media. A lie can travel around the world and back again while the truth is lacing up its boots.

Unfortunately, we cannot rely on the government at present to take strict action to curb misinformation or to strengthen citizen journalism. Because the government is busy using our screentime to spread to break down everything citizen journalism stands for.

I deeply appreciate Amal for choosing such a timely and relevant topic for his book. In an era where the lines between media and public voices are constantly evolving, his focus on citizen journalism and the public sphere couldn't be more pertinent. This work goes beyond merely documenting a phenomenon; it captures the essence of how ordinary individuals, armed with smartphones and conviction, are reshaping the narrative of truth and accountability.

I'm genuinely proud of this effort and look forward to seeing the impact it will have on readers and society at large. This book is more than a contribution to academic discourse – it's a call to action for a more empowered and connected world.

Sahaya Novinston Lobo

Senior Crime Reporter,

The New Indian Express, Chennai, Tamil Nadu.

"Is India becoming a dictatorship?" This was the title which featured in a video posted by a young man named Dhruv Rathi on his YouTube channel on February 22, 2024. Dhruv Rathi, known for questioning government policies with data-driven analysis, stands as a remarkable example of what citizen journalism can and should aspire to be.

The internet, mobile phones, and social media have ushered in a new era, disrupting the traditional media landscape. Citizen journalism has emerged as the "fifth estate," offering an alternative to the conventional "fourth pillar" of democracy. Ordinary individuals have become journalists, reporting on developments around them without the privileges or institutional backing of traditional media. They seek opinions, share insights, and present their perspectives—often with a vigor and authenticity that surpass mainstream media.

Critics argue that journalism cannot be practiced merely by wielding a mobile camera. Yet, in today's world, even young children with a smartphone and a social media account can create impactful journalistic content. Across the globe, from war zones to local communities, we witness such examples every day. Consider how Dhruv Rathi, with his relentless pursuit of facts and nuanced commentary, has challenged the dominance of traditional media. Often, stories uncovered by citizen journalists are later amplified by the mainstream media, proving the former's critical role in today's information ecosystem.

The media industry is currently grappling with an internal conflict: on one side, traditional media professionals; on the other, everyday citizens armed with mobile cameras. This competition has created fluctuations and debates about journalistic authenticity and responsibility. However, it is undeniable that citizen journalism has become an essential element of democracy in this age of digital connectivity. Despite its flaws and limitations, it plays a vital role in ensuring diverse voices are heard.

In this context, my friend Amal's book, Citizen Journalism, holds immense significance. It is both a tribute and a guide for citizen journalists who, without any formal credentials, tirelessly document the realities around them. The book maps the journey of citizen journalism, highlighting its transformative potential and challenges. Amal, as an author, delves deeply into the human mind, parallel to his own intellectual explorations.

May this book serve as a cornerstone in the study of citizen journalism and inspire countless others to embrace the spirit of independent reporting.

Jomit Jose

Senior Sub Editor,

Asianet News, Trivandrum, Kerala.

In an age where every individual has the potential to become a storyteller, citizen journalism has emerged as a powerful force, redefining the way we consume and understand news. This book offers a compelling exploration of how everyday citizens in India are not only reporting but also shaping public discourse, bridging the gap between traditional media and grassroots realities.

With a keen eye for detail and a deep understanding of media dynamics, the author unravels the complexities of the Citizen Journalism, the so called 'Fifth Estate,' shedding light on its transformative impact on democracy and the public sphere. This work is not just a study of citizen journalism—it is a tribute to the power of the human voice in the digital age.

Congratulations to Mr. Amal for choosing such a timely and relevant topic for his book. In an era where the lines between traditional media and citizen voices are increasingly blurred, this work promises to offer valuable insights into the role of citizen journalism in shaping public discourse. Best wishes for its success and impact!

Dr. Gnana D Hans

Assistant Professor,

Department of Communication,

Manonmaniam Sundaranar University, Tirunelveli, Tamil Nadu.

Throughout the long walks with Amal from the second gate to Silver Jubilee campus of Pondicherry University, our discussion about *people* have reached to a promising culmination. This book is alive. He has extensively written about citizen journalism, and he has summoned it into being, with every chapter pulsing the threads of our discussions on his thoughts. When he first spoke to me about this book, it felt less like a book and more like a map that trace several constellations of his thoughts on citizen journalism.

Here, you will find more than history or theory. You will see how a smartphone transforms into a lens for truth, how you can carry a weapon powerful than an AK-47 in your hand, and how the simplest act of speaking up can bring revolution, how a common person reshapes what we understand as power. The book opens into the global stage and then brings us home to India, through raw stories.

This work reminds us that the public sphere is not some distant concept, rather a space we perform our every day, to act, to question and to evolve. The chapters show not only what citizen journalism is but what it could become. It thus is as much a guide as a call to action, provoke every reader to impersonate one's social responsibility. Read a rare reflection of this restless era, rendered with social touch.

This is the voice of countless people. Read, act, and join the chorus.

Dr. Ameer Salman OM

Assistant Professor and Head,

Department of Mass Communication and Journalism,

Farook College (Autonomous), Kozhikode, Kerala.

With a smartphone in almost everyone's pocket, we all now have the power to become storytellers and reporters, capturing the world as it unfolds around us. Imagine witnessing something incredible or important. In seconds, you can record a video, snap a photo, or write a quick post and share it with the world. Social media platforms, news websites, and even personal blogs provide the stage for us to broadcast our perspectives, instantly turning us into citizen journalists.

This approach to journalism is revolutionizing traditional media in the best ways. It's no longer only one side of the story. We're hearing from a wider range of voices. Stories from marginalized communities, local events, and unique perspectives are now being shared, making the news more inclusive and representative.

Choosing citizen journalism as a career is also much easier now if you're passionate about certain issues or have a knack for storytelling. Many news outlets are eager for fresh content from freelance contributors. You can get paid for your stories, photos, and videos. You can build a following and become an influential voice in your niche, all while being your own boss.

The write up from my dearest senior Mr. Amal Jith Raveendran takes you on an incredible journey into the world of citizen journalism and how it amplifying people's voice. This book also highlights the courage and determination of individuals who, despite the odds, strive to make a difference. Their stories are a reminder that each of us has the power to impact the world in meaningful ways. Happy reading!

Anju S Kunjumon

Assistant Producer,

OnManorama, Kochi, Kerala.

It is a big privilege as well as a profound honor to write the foreword for "Citizen Journalism and Public Sphere: Unveiling the Power of People's Voice", a book written by my close friend Amal Jith Raveendran, whom I happened to meet at the National Media Conclave held in Bhubaneswar. It was that fortuitous meeting that marked the beginning of an intellectual partnership based on mutual enthusiasm for journalism, communication, and the transformative influence of narrative.

The topic covered within this book, citizen journalism, is of great significance in the current media landscape. Given the conventional news organizations' troubles with scarce resources, biases, and greater public scrutiny, the phenomenon of citizen journalists being called the "Fifth Estate" throws up new themes on storytelling, dissemination, and reception. This volume adequately addresses the unfolding of citizen journalism, its powerful ability to democratize information, and the role that citizen journalism plays as an oversight mechanism against mainstream media and powerful establishments. What gives this study a comparative edge is the fair-minded way in which dual-faceted characteristics of citizen journalism are considered.

While advocating for its capacity to amplify the voices of marginalized groups, foster accountability, and oppose established narratives, Amal candidly addresses its attendant ethical, legal, and practical challenges. A critical look at issues ranging from how misinformation is spread through these newsgathering technologies can benefit readers in understanding this highly emerging field. Using a variety of global and local case studies, the book situates citizen journalism in its many historical, cultural, and technological contexts. It makes powerful claims for its importance in salient international events like the Arab Spring and Black Lives Matter and its role in key periods in India's past on how ordinary citizens have changed the public sphere, brought social change, and kept governments accountable. My appreciation for the author's dedication and analytical depth has grown with each conversation we have had. His ability to seamlessly weave personal views with academic research and practical examples makes this book accessible yet profoundly insightful. It is more than a story about the rise of the Fifth Estate; it is a call to action for citizens, journalists, and policymakers to embrace its power while responsibly addressing its limitations.

This is an important and timely contribution toward the continuing discussion over issues with contemporary journalism and democratic principles. Its pages, I hope, will be viewed by readers both as a resource and as a challenge, marshalling them to reimagine lines of journalism's reach and the responsibility of individuals in moving a literate society toward justice.

As you interact with these materials, I implore you to reflect on the meaning of citizen's voice and the responsibility that comes with its exercise. Together, let us strive toward a new era of storytelling as being both democratized and instrumental for telling the truth, delivering justice, and improving the collective.

Adrash HS

Research Scholar,

Department of Political Scienece,

Kerala University, Trivandrum, Kerala.

Through countless talks spiced by the tangy lemon-teas and the idyllic bliss of Pondicherry University, one thing that stood out about Amal is his clarity of thoughts and his unwavering commitment to the ethos he holds for. Now, to see those powerful thoughts distilled into a promising book feels like a long-cherished dream coming true. It fills me with profound joy and anticipation to write this foreword for you, man!

To start with, Amal's work on Citizen Journalism is a fresh take sweeping through a well-trodden trail. His new perspectives and sharp insights cut through the noise and offer a compelling narrative. What he brings to the table is not just an analysis but an unconventional approach that reshapes how we understand and practice Citizen Journalism.

Amal's work resonates with the core of the common man and rightly captures how a mere smartphone can transform into a lens for truth. He takes us through compelling stories that capture the true transformative potential of Citizen Journalism. These chapters don't just explain what Citizen Journalism is; they explore what it could become – a guide, a provocation, and a call to embrace our shared social responsibility.

I urge you to see Amal's world through his work. I'm sure you'll find not just knowledge there, but inspiration – a reminder that in the simplest acts of speaking up lies the power to change the world.

Ann Chris Fernandez

Instructional Designer,

Skill-up Technologies, New Delhi, India.

In an age where information is readily available and accessible, the role of the citizen journalist has never been more important. Amal's book, "Citizen Journalism and Public Sphere: Unveiling the Power of the People's Voice", delves deep into this dynamic landscape, exploring how ordinary individuals are shaping the narrative of our times.

I first encountered Amal Jith Raveendran at the National Media Conclave in Bhubaneswar. His passion for journalism and storytelling was palpable, a spark that ignited conversations that spanned the realms of fiction and politics. As a fellow research scholar in Political science, I was immediately impressed by his insightful observations and keen understanding of the media's role in shaping public discourse.

 In "Citizen Journalism and Public Sphere: Unveiling the Power of the People's Voice", Amal continues to impress. His deep understanding of the media landscape and his ability to articulate complex ideas with clarity make this book a compelling read. It's a testament to his talent and dedication throughout the years. Amal offers a comprehensive and timely analysis of the evolving media landscape. His ability to bridge the gap between academic theory and real-world practice is commendable.

Through his insightful analysis and compelling case studies, Amal highlights the transformative potential of citizen journalism. He demonstrates how empowered citizens, armed with smartphones and social media, can hold institutions accountable, amplify marginalized voices, and foster a more informed and engaged public sphere. This book is a timely and essential read for anyone interested in the future of journalism, media studies, and civic engagement. It offers a nuanced understanding of the challenges and opportunities that lie ahead for citizen journalists and the broader public.

I encourage you to embark on this thought-provoking journey with Amal, as he unravels the power of the people's voice and its impact on our society. I am confident that this book will not only inspire budding journalists but also spark important conversations about the role of the media in shaping our society.

Revathy C

Research Scholar,

Department of Political Scienece,

Kerala University, Trivandrum, Kerala.

As I write this foreword to Amal Jith Raveendran sir's remarkable book, I am filled with a sense of admiration and respect for the author's tireless dedication to exploring the complex and multifaceted world of citizen journalism. His book is a comprehensive and insightful exploration of the world of citizen journalism. Through his meticulous research and analysis, the author sheds light on the power, potential, and challenges of citizen journalism, and its impact on democratic societies.

In India, the legal framework governing citizen journalism is still evolving. The Indian Constitution guarantees the right to freedom of speech and expression under Article 19(1)(a), which includes the right to receive and impart information. However, this right is not absolute and is subject to reasonable restrictions imposed by the state.

The Information Technology Act, 2000, and the Rules framed thereunder, provide a framework for regulating online content, including citizen journalism. However, the Act and the Rules have been criticized for being overly broad and vague, and for failing to provide adequate protections for freedom of speech and expression.

From a legal perspective, citizen journalism raises several important questions. For instance, what are the implications of citizen journalism for traditional notions of journalism and the role of the journalist? How do we balance the need for free speech and expression with the need for accuracy and accountability in citizen journalism? What are the legal implications of citizen journalism for issues such as defamation, libel, and copyright infringement?

Throughout this book, writer conveys that citizen journalism has the potential to democratize information and empower marginalized voices. By providing a platform for individuals to share their stories and perspectives, citizen journalism can help to create a more inclusive and diverse media landscape.

I would like to extend my sincerest appreciation to Amal Jith Raveendran sir for his outstanding work, and for his commitment to exploring the complex issues and themes that are at the heart of this book. His dedication to the subject matter is evident throughout the book, and his insights and analysis have significantly contributed to our understanding of the role of citizen journalism in shaping democratic societies.

Sreegeeth Raveend

Law Student,

Mumbai University, Mumbai.

Preface

In the 2013 blockbuster movie *Chennai Express*, Shah Rukh Khan delivers a dialogue that resonates beyond cinema: *"Never underestimate the power of a common man."* These words perfectly encapsulate the essence of citizen journalism – a phenomenon that empowers ordinary individuals to challenge the status quo, uncover hidden truths, and reshape the contours of the public sphere.

The idea of writing this book, *Citizen Journalism and Public Sphere: Unveiling the Power of the People's Voice,* first took shape in February 2023 when I was invited by the Department of Journalism at Majilis Arts and Science College, Malappuram, to deliver an invited talk. My topic was the evolving trends and future of citizen journalism. The interactive session that followed proved to be a pivotal moment. The enthusiasm, questions, and fresh ideas shared by the students inspired me to delve deeper into this subject. It became evident that the rising tide of citizen journalism deserved a comprehensive exploration – one that documented its current trajectory while envisioning its future potential.

This book is the result of nearly one and a half years of research, writing, and introspection. During this period, I immersed myself in understanding the theoretical foundations, practical implications, and societal impact of citizen journalism. The journey also involved studying global and local examples of how ordinary individuals are shaping public discourse. From social media platforms to grassroots movements, citizen journalism has emerged as a force to reckon with in today's interconnected world.

The influence of figures like Dhruv Rathee, who has become a torchbearer of citizen journalism in India, cannot be overstated.

His ability to blend facts with compelling narratives has opened new dimensions in this space. Today, we see countless individuals – armed with mobile phones and the internet – rising to challenge inequalities, highlight injustices, and demand accountability. This surge of grassroots voices exemplifies the true spirit of democracy and underscores the immense power of the common man.

Citizen journalism is not without its challenges. Questions about credibility, biases, and the misuse of digital platforms often surface. Yet, its potential to democratize information and amplify marginalized voices outweighs these concerns. The very essence of citizen journalism lies in its inclusivity – anyone, regardless of their background or resources, can participate in the narrative – building process. This inclusivity strengthens our democracy and makes it more participatory.

Through this book, I aim to provide a holistic understanding of citizen journalism, tracing its evolution, analyzing its impact on the public sphere, and exploring the ethical dilemmas it presents. The book seeks to address pressing questions: How does citizen journalism coexist with traditional media? What are its limitations? How can it be leveraged to create a more informed and equitable society?

Writing this book has been a humbling experience. It allowed me to reflect on how far we have come in the realm of participatory media and how much further we can go. It has also reinforced my belief in the power of collective voices to bring about meaningful change.

As you read this book, I hope it sparks curiosity and inspires you to think critically about the role of citizen journalism in our lives. Whether you are a student, an academic, a media professional, or an active participant in the public sphere, this book is for you.

Your thoughts, feedback, suggestions, and criticisms are invaluable, as they will enrich this dialogue and contribute to the evolving discourse on citizen journalism.

I am honored to be a small part of this vibrant and ever-expanding public sphere. May this book encourage more individuals to embrace the spirit of citizen journalism and wield the power of the people's voice responsibly.

Happy reading!

- Amal Jith Raveendran

CHAPTER 1

AN INTRODUCTION TO CITIZEN JOURNALISM

1. Citizen Journalism

Citizen journalism refers to the practice of ordinary people, who are not professional journalists, participating in the creation and dissemination of news content. It involves the use of social media, blogs and other digital platforms to report on events and share information with others.

Citizen journalists may cover a wide range of topics from local news and incidents to political rallies and protests. They may also capture and share photos and videos of numerous breaking news as they unfold, usually providing unique perspectives and eyewitness accounts.

The rise of citizen journalism has been fuelled by the widespread adoption of mobile technology and the democratization of access to information – standardization of knowledge. With the ability to capture and share news content from their smartphones, ordinary people now have the power to act as reporters, bringing attention to issues that may not have otherwise received coverage in traditional media outlets.

While citizen journalism has the potential to provide valuable contributions to the public discourse, it is important to note the challenges that they undertake. Citizen journalists may lack the training, expertise and resources of professional journalists, which can lead to inaccuracies or biases in their reporting. Moreover, the spread of fake news and disinformation through social media has highlighted the need for careful evaluation of sources and details provided.

This phenomenon has emerged in recent years due to the widespread availability of digital tools and platforms that allow anyone with a smartphone and an internet connection to announce particulars on occurrences and disseminate information with the audience.

The rise of citizen journalism can be attributed to several factors. First, the democratization of access to information has made it possible for people from all walks of life to have a voice and share their perspectives with a global audience. Social media platforms like Twitter, Facebook and Instagram have provided a space for citizen journalists to connect with others and share their stories, breaking news and eyewitness accounts.

Another factor that has contributed to the rise of citizen journalism is the decline of traditional news media. Many people have become disillusioned with mainstream news sources and are turning to citizen journalists for more diverse and authentic perspectives. Moreover, citizen journalists frequently cover issues that are overlooked or ignored by traditional news outlets such as local events, community and social justice concerns.

Citizen journalism has become a conspicuous force in the media landscape. It has played a crucial role in documenting social movements and political protests and has helped to bring attention to remarkable matters that may have otherwise been overlooked by traditional news sources. Citizen journalism has the potential to promote greater transparency and accountability in the media by providing a counterbalance to traditional news outlets and holding them to higher standards of reporting.

Citizen journalism represents a significant shift in the way that news is produced and consumed. The democratization of access to and the rise of digital platforms have given ordinary people the power to act as reporters and bring attention to subjects that matter to them. As such, citizen journalism is a noteworthy development in the media landscape and is likely to continue to wield an appreciable position in shaping public opinion and promoting transparency in the media.

2. History of Citizen Journalism

Citizen journalism has a long and rich history that dates back to ancient times. People have always had a desire to share news and information with others, and throughout history, they have used various means to do so. The term "citizen journalism" itself is a relatively recent development, but the concept of non-professionals participating in the creation and dissemination of news content has been around for centuries.

In ancient times, people used various means to communicate tidings and information including town criers, who would shout news and announcements in public places. The invention of the printing press by Johannes Guttenberg in the 15th century marked a significant turning point for citizen journalism as it made it possible for people to publish and distribute their own news content. This led to the emergence of newspapers and pamphlets that were written and published by non-professionals. These publications usually focused on domestic news and happenings, providing a valuable source of information for their communities.

In ancient Greece, the concept of democracy was closely tied to citizens' participation in government affairs. Citizens were encouraged to engage in public discourse and share their opinions on political matters. This ethos extended to the dissemination of news and information as people would gather in public spaces to discuss contemporary affairs and exchange details with each other.

In the 18th century, the American Revolution pronounced a pivotal moment for citizen journalism. The proliferation of newspapers and pamphlets played a key role in shaping public opinion and rallying support for the revolution. Citizens wrote and published their own news content, providing an alternative to the heavily-controlled British newspapers.

The 19th and early 20th centuries saw the rise of the penny press, which made newspapers more accessible to the masses. This led to the emergence of a new breed of citizen journalists, who wrote for and edited penny papers. These newspapers regularly focused on sensational stories and gossip, but they also covered important news and events that were of interest to the public.

The 20th century witnessed the rise of radio and television that brought news and information into the vicinity of people's homes. However, these mediums were largely controlled by a small group of professionals, and it was difficult for non-professionals to participate in the modelling of news content.

The emergence of the internet in the 1990s can be regarded as a milestone in citizen journalism as it empowered individuals to publish and share their own contents. This led to the rise of blogs, which allowed people to create and publish their own news and opinions without the need for traditional news outlets. The rise of social media in the 2000s marked another turning point for citizen journalism, as it provided a space for non-professionals to share news and information with others on a global scale.

3. Internet and Citizen Journalism

The internet has been a game-changer in the world of journalism, especially with the growth of citizen journalism. Citizen journalists started reporting on events and news, usually through social media and other online channels. The internet has urged anyone with an internet connection to publish and distribute their stories, bypassing traditional gatekeepers of the news industry.

One of the biggest impacts of the internet on citizen journalism is the democratization of the news process. In the past, news was largely controlled by a small number of major news outlets, which had the resources to send reporters around the world to cover important events. However, with the internet, anyone can now document occurrences and share their stories with a global audience. This has given rise to a new wave of citizen journalists who are able to outmanoeuvre conventional guardians and provide a different perspective on events.

The internet has also made it easier for citizen journalists to disseminate their stories to a wider audience. In the past, citizen journalists were limited to publishing their stories in local newspapers or distributing them via word of mouth. With the advent of the internet, citizen journalists can now share their stories with a global audience via social media platforms, blogs, and other online channels such as Facebook, Twitter and YouTube etc. This has enabled citizens to reach a much larger audience than was previously possible and has given them a powerful tool for influencing public opinion.

Internet empowered citizens to connect with one another. Social media platforms such as Twitter, Facebook and Instagram have made it easy for citizens to form networks and divulge information mutually. This has enabled citizens to collaborate on stories and provide a more comprehensive coverage of events.

4. The 'Fifth Estate'

Citizen journalism has been referred to as the fifth estate because it represents a powerful alternative to the traditional four estates of democracy: The Legislature, Judiciary, Executive and the Media. Citizen journalism has the potential to act as a watchdog, monitoring and scrutinizing the actions of those in power, and providing a platform for diverse voices and perspectives.

The traditional media has long been considered the fourth estate, acting as a critical watchdog of government and other powerful institutions. But, with the rise of citizen journalism, the media's monopoly on news and information has been challenged. Citizen journalists generally have a deeper understanding of the issues affecting their communities, and their reporting can provide a more accurate and thoughtful portrayal of events.

The term "fifth estate" refers to a group or class outside of the traditional power structures of government, the media and big business. Citizen journalism has emerged as a powerful force in this fifth estate, providing an alternative source of news and information to the mainstream media. Citizen journalists are regularly able to provide a more personal and nuanced perspective on incidents, which can help to fill in the gaps left by traditional news reporting.

Citizen journalists are commonly the ones who uncover stories of corruption, abuse of power and other wrongdoing. They can shine a light on these problems and bring them to the attention of the wider public. This helps to ensure that those in power are held accountable for their actions and that the public is informed about important cases that may otherwise have gone unnoticed.

5. Types of Citizen Journalism

There are several types of citizen journalism, including:

i) Observational Citizen Journalism: This type of citizen journalism involves individuals capturing and reporting on events and experiences as they happen, usually using their smartphones or other digital devices to capture images and videos of events.

ii) Opinion-Based Citizen Journalism: This type of citizen journalism entails individuals who share their opinions and perspectives on news and current events, frequently through social media or personal blogs.

iii) Participatory Citizen Journalism: This type of citizen journalism encompasses individuals actively participating in the news-gathering process by contributing to crowd sourced reporting projects or sharing information and tips with journalists.

iv) Collaborative Citizen Journalism: This type of citizen journalism comprises individuals working together to investigate or report on a particular issue or story, continually through online collaboration tools or networks.

v) Investigative Citizen Journalism: This type of citizen journalism incorporates individuals investigating and reporting on situations or stories that may be overlooked or ignored by traditional news organizations, encompassing in-depth research and analysis to uncover hidden information or expose wrongdoing.

Each type of citizen journalism has its own strengths and weaknesses, and they can contribute to a more informed and engaged public by providing a more diverse range of perspectives and voices in the news media. Nevertheless, it's important for citizen journalists to follow proper journalistic standards and to be aware of the risks and challenges associated with this type of reporting.

6. Observational Citizen Journalism

Observational citizen journalism is a form of reporting where individuals capture and report on events and experiences as they happen. This type of journalism is based on first-hand observation and documentation of events rather than relying on secondary sources or hearsay. Observational citizen journalists repeatedly use their smartphones or other digital devices to capture images and videos of events, which they then share through social media or other online platforms.

Observational citizen journalism is different from traditional news reporting, which relies on professional journalists and news organizations to gather and report on events. Observational citizen journalism allows ordinary people to participate in the reporting and documentation of events, and can provide a unique outlook on events that may be missed or underreported by traditional news outlets.

It consents for a more diverse range of approaches and voices to be heard. Traditional news outlets generally have their own biases and perspectives, which can limit the range of viewpoints presented. Observational citizen journalists, on the other hand, come from all walks of life and may have different priorities and perspectives. This can provide a more nuanced and multifaceted understanding of events.

Observational citizen journalism can also be a powerful tool for holding those in power accountable. By documenting events as they happen, citizen journalists can shine a light on wrongdoing or injustices that might otherwise go unnoticed. This can help to spur action and change, and hold those in power accountable for their actions.

But, there are also some challenges and risks associated with observational citizen journalism. For example, there is a risk of false or misleading information being spread if citizen journalists do not fact-check their observations or rely on unverified sources. There is also a risk of safety concerns if citizen journalists put themselves in harm's way in order to capture an event.

7. Opinion-Based Citizen Journalism

Opinion-based citizen journalism is a form of reporting where individuals share their personal opinions and view point on a particular topic or issue. This type of journalism is different from traditional news reporting which is typically based on facts and objectivity. It allows people to express their standpoints and to engage in public discourse in a more informal and personal way.

Opinion-based citizen journalism can take many different forms, including blog posts, social media updates, podcasts and video content. The content produced by opinion citizen journalists can cover a wide range of topics from politics and current events to entertainment and culture. In many cases, opinion citizen journalists focus on niche topics that might not be covered by mainstream media outlets.

This type of citizen journalism allows individuals to share their distinctive point of views and to contribute to public discourse in a more democratic way. By sharing their opinions, citizen journalists can add to the diversity of opinions on a particular issue and can help to create a more nuanced and multifaceted understanding of complex topics.

A challenge associated with it is that it can be difficult to separate fact from opinion, especially when opinions are presented as if they are factual. This can lead to the spread of false or misleading information which can be harmful to public discourse.

To ensure that opinion-based citizen journalism is done effectively, it's important for citizen journalists to clearly distinguish between their opinions and facts. They should also strive to present a balanced view of the topic and to acknowledge alternative perspectives. By doing so, citizen journalists can help create a more informed and engaged public.

8. Participatory Citizen Journalism

In participatory citizen journalism individuals actively join in the news-gathering process. This can include contributing to crowd sourced reporting projects, sharing information and tips with journalists or using social media to share eyewitness accounts of news events.

Participatory citizen journalism can take many different forms such as citizen photojournalism, where individuals use their smartphones to capture images and videos of news events, or crowdsourcing, where individuals contribute information, research and insights to a larger reporting project.

Participatory citizen journalism contributes to democratizing the news media by allowing a more diverse range of perspectives and voices to be heard. By involving ordinary citizens in the news-gathering process, participatory citizen journalism can help break down traditional barriers between journalists and their audiences and create a more collaborative and engaged relationship.

It can also help fill gaps in traditional news coverage, particularly in areas where there may be limited access to mainstream media. By using social media and other digital tools to share information and insights, citizens can help shed light on important issues that may be overlooked or ignored by traditional news organizations.

9. Collaborative Citizen Journalism

In collaborative citizen journalism, individuals work together to investigate or report on a particular issue or story. This type of citizen journalism involves using online collaboration tools or networks to share information, research and perspectives.

Collaborative citizen journalism can take many forms such as crowdsourcing information, collaborating on investigative reporting projects or creating community-based news outlets. The goal of collaborative citizen journalism is to harness the power of collective intelligence and collaboration to produce high-quality, accurate reporting on major issues.

It allows for a more diverse range of attitudes and voices to be heard. By working together, individuals can share their idiosyncratic encounters and expertise, leading to a more refined and comprehensive understanding of complex issues.

Collaborative citizen journalism can also be a powerful tool for community building and social change. By working together, individuals can create a sense of shared purpose and ownership over the news media, which can help build trust and engagement among community members.

10. Investigative Citizen Journalism

Investigative citizen journalism is a type of reporting where individuals explore and report on issues or stories that may be overlooked or ignored by traditional news organizations. This type of journalism involves in-depth research, interviews and analysis to uncover hidden information or expose wrongdoing.

Investigative citizen journalists usually use a variety of sources and techniques to gather information and corroborate their findings. This may include public records requests, Freedom of Information Act (FOIA) requests, data analysis and interviews with sources. The goal of investigative citizen journalism is to discover chief information that can apprise the public and hold those in power liable.

Investigative citizen journalists are commonly motivated by a desire to expose the truth and to hold those in power accountable, which can lead to a more comprehensive and subtle understanding of sophisticated matters.

It can also be a powerful tool for social and political change. By exposing wrongdoing or bringing attention to vital concerns, investigative citizen journalists can help spur action and change. They can also give a voice to marginalized or underrepresented communities and can help shine a light on issues that might otherwise be ignored.

11. Skills Needed for a Citizen Journalist

Citizen journalists require certain skills to effectively navigate the world of news reporting and storytelling. Here are some essential skills for citizen journalists:

i) Journalism Ethics and Standards: Citizen journalists must understand and adhere to basic journalistic principles such as accuracy, fairness and impartiality. They should have a strong understanding of media ethics, including the importance of fact-checking, verifying sources and maintaining journalistic integrity. Adhering to these standards ensures that citizen journalists produce credible and trustworthy content.

ii) News Gathering and Research: Being able to gather information and conduct thorough research is crucial for citizen journalists. They should possess the ability to identify reliable sources, collect accurate data and fact-check information before reporting it. Effective research skills enable citizen journalists to provide context, background and a comprehensive understanding of the topics they cover.

iii) Interviewing and Communication: Interviewing skills are essential for citizen journalists when gathering firsthand accounts or conducting expert interviews. They should be able to ask relevant and probing questions, listen actively and create a comfortable environment for interviewees to share their perspectives. Strong communication skills - both verbal and written - allow citizen journalists to present information vividly and engage their audience efficaciously.

iv) Storytelling and Narrative Building: Citizen journalists need to craft compelling narratives that resonate with their audience. They should be able to identify key elements of a story, structure their reports effectively and seize readers or viewers through powerful storytelling techniques. Developing a narrative that captivates the audience helps citizen journalists convey their message and impact public opinion.

v) Visual and Multimedia Skills: As citizen journalism increasingly relies on multimedia content, having visual and multimedia skills is essential. Citizen journalists should understand the basics of photography and videography inclusive of composition lighting and framing. They should be able to capture impactful visuals that enhance their storytelling.

Additionally, knowledge of video editing, graphics creation and multimedia production enables citizen journalists to present their stories in a visually appealing and compelling manner.

vi) Critical Thinking and Objectivity: Citizen journalists should possess critical thinking skills to analyze complex issues, identify biases and evaluate the credibility of sources. They should strive to present multiple stances and maintain objectivity in their reporting. The ability to think judiciously and impartially ensures citizen journalists provide well-rounded and balanced coverage, enabling their audience to form informed opinions.

vii) Adaptability and Resilience: The landscape of citizen journalism is evolving persistently. Citizen journalists must be adaptable and willing to learn new tools, technologies and storytelling methods. They must also be resilient as they may face challenges, criticism or backlash for their work. The ability to adapt and bounce back from setbacks allows citizen journalists to continue making meaningful contributions to the field.

Becoming a successful citizen journalist demands a range of skills like journalistic ethics, research abilities, effective communication skills, storytelling techniques, visual and multimedia proficiency, adaptability and resilience. By honing these skills, citizen journalists can make a salient impact by bringing diverse perspectives, raising awareness and fostering positive change in the world of news reporting.

12. Tools and Equipment for Citizen Journalists on the Go

To engage effectively in citizen journalism, certain tools and equipment are essential. There are a variety of key tools and equipment required for citizen journalists to successfully gather, create, and disseminate news.

i) Smartphone: The smartphone is the most indispensable tool for citizen journalists on the go. With high-quality cameras, audio recording capabilities and internet connectivity, smartphones allow for quick and convenient news gathering. They permit citizen journalists to capture photos and videos, conduct interviews, record audio and instantly share content through social media platforms. Smartphones also offer access to various news apps, research tools and communication channels, keeping citizen journalists connected and informed.

ii) Portable Digital Camera: While smartphones have advanced camera capabilities, a portable digital camera can provide citizen journalists with enhanced control and quality. Compact cameras with high-resolution sensors, optical zoom and manual settings allow for professional-grade photography. These cameras are lightweight, easily portable and offer superior image quality, making them ideal for capturing events, portraits or visual evidence while in transit.

iii) Lightweight Video Camera or Action Camera: For citizen journalists who focus on video reporting, a lightweight video camera or action camera is a valuable asset. These cameras are compact, durable and designed to capture high-quality video footage in various conditions. They are particularly useful for capturing action-packed scenes or events that require hands-free recording. With features such as image stabilization and wide-angle lenses, they ensure steady and immersive video documentation.

iv) Portable Audio Recorder: Clear and reliable audio is essential for successful storytelling. A portable audio recorder provides citizen journalists with the ability to capture high-quality sound on the go. These compact devices offer improved audio control, noise reduction features and external microphone options, ensuring that interviews, ambient sounds or voiceovers are recorded with precision. Portable audio recorders facilitate citizen journalists to enhance the audio quality of their reports, adding depth and authenticity to their stories.

v) Lightweight Tripod or Stabilizer: Stability is crucial when capturing photos or videos while in transit. A lightweight tripod or stabilizer helps citizen journalists maintain steady shots and prevent blurring by improving visual quality. Compact tripods or handheld stabilizers are designed for portability, allowing for stable footage even in dynamic or fast-paced environments. They are versatile tools that enable citizen journalists to create professional-looking visuals while maintaining flexibility and mobility.

vi) Portable Power Bank: A reliable power source is a necessity for citizen journalists in motion. A portable power bank serves as a backup power supply for smartphones, cameras and other electronic devices. It allows citizen journalists to recharge their devices when traditional power outlets are unavailable, ensuring they can continue reporting without the worry of running out of battery. Portable power banks come in several capacities and sizes, providing extended power options for extended reporting sessions.

vii) Mobile Internet Hotspot: To stay connected and share stories in real-time, citizen journalists require a stable internet connection. A mobile internet hotspot allows them to create their Wi-Fi network, providing internet access to their devices even in remote locations or areas with limited connectivity. Mobile hotspots ensure that citizen journalists can quickly upload content, engage with their audience and access online resources while on the go, enhancing their ability to report in real-time.

viii) Portable External Hard Drive: When covering events or traveling extensively, citizen journalists may accumulate a significant amount of multimedia content. A portable external hard drive provides additional storage capacity for backing up and organizing media files. These devices are compact, lightweight and durable.

ix) Mobile Editing Apps and Software: Editing and post-production are vital stages in creating compelling news content. Mobile editing apps and software enable citizen journalists to edit photos and videos directly on their smartphones or tablets. These intuitive applications provide basic editing tools, filters, transitions and even advanced features like colour grading or audio mixing. Mobile editing apps empower citizen journalists to produce polished and engaging content while in action, saving time and eliminating the need for bulky editing equipment.

x) Portable Wireless Microphone: High-quality audio is essential for interviews and video reports. A portable wireless microphone system allows citizen journalists to capture clear and professional-grade audio from a distance. These compact microphones typically consist of a transmitter and receiver, providing freedom of movement and flexibility during interviews or recording sessions. Portable wireless microphones ensure that citizen journalists can capture pristine audio even in noisy or crowded environments.

xi) Personal Safety and First Aid Kit: The safety and well-being of citizen journalists are paramount. Carrying a personal safety kit, including items such as a first aid kit, emergency contact information, personal protective equipment and essential supplies, is crucial for their physical and mental well-being. These kits help citizen journalists mitigate risks, address minor injuries and stay prepared for unexpected situations while travelling.

By leveraging these tools, citizen journalists can contribute to a more inclusive and diverse media landscape, amplifying voices, shedding light on underreported stories and fostering a greater understanding of the world around us. As technology continues to evolve, it is fundamental for citizen journalists to stay updated and adapt to emerging tools and techniques, further enhancing the reliability and influence of their work.

13. Essential Apps for Citizen Journalism

In the digital era, mobile applications have become indispensable tools for citizen journalists. These apps provide citizen journalists with the ability to capture, edit and disseminate news content on the go. With the convenience and accessibility they offer, mobile apps empower citizen journalists to report in real-time and engage with their audience meritoriously.

i) Social Media Platforms: Social media platforms such as Twitter, Facebook, Instagram and YouTube are powerful tools for citizen journalists to share news content quickly and reach a wide audience. These platforms allow citizen journalists to post updates, share photos and videos and engage in real-time conversations. They facilitate the distribution of news content, enable citizen journalists to connect with their followers and promote dialogue and awareness around urgent issues.

ii) Mobile Journalism Apps: Mobile journalism (MoJo) apps provide a range of features for citizen journalists to create professional-looking content directly from their smartphones. These apps generally include video editing tools, filters, overlays and audio enhancements. Popular MoJo apps like Filmic Pro, LumaFusion or Adobe Premiere Rush allow citizen journalists to shoot, edit and share high-quality videos without the need for specialized equipment or software.

iii) Live Streaming Apps: Live streaming apps such as Periscope, Facebook Live or YouTube Live, enable citizen journalists to broadcast real-time video coverage of happenings or breaking news stories. These apps provide an immersive experience for viewers, allowing them to witness events as they unfold. Live streaming apps enhance citizen journalists' ability to share raw, unfiltered footage and occupy with their audience in real-time through comments and interactions.

iv) News Aggregator Apps: News aggregator apps, such as Flipboard, Feedly or Google News are valuable tools for citizen journalists to stay updated on current events and access a variety of news sources. These apps curate personalized news feeds based on user preferences, providing a diverse range of articles, videos and multimedia content. News aggregator apps enable citizen journalists to stay informed, discover new stories and gather information from multiple sources, enhancing the accuracy and depth of their reporting.

v) Photography Apps: Photography apps, such as Snapseed, VSCO or Adobe Lightroom offer powerful editing tools and filters to enhance and optimize photos captured by citizen journalists. These apps provide options for adjusting exposure, contrast, colour and adding creative effects. Photography apps enable citizen journalists to produce visually enchanting images that convey their stories effectually, enhancing the impact of their reporting.

vi) Audio Recording and Editing Apps: Audio recording and editing apps such as Voice Memos, Audacity or Anchor are essential for citizen journalists to capture and edit high-quality audio content. These apps offer features like noise reduction, equalization and audio trimming, enabling citizen journalists to produce clear and professional-grade audio recordings. Audio recording and editing apps enrich the storytelling experience by improving the quality of interviews, ambient sounds or voiceovers.

vii) Mapping and Geolocation Apps: Mapping and geolocation apps such as Google Maps, Geotag Photos Pro or Mapillary assist citizen journalists in providing accurate location information and visual context to their stories. These apps allow citizen journalists to geotag their photos and videos, providing geographical context and helping audience understand the location-specific aspects of a story. Mapping and geolocation apps enhance the credibility and relevance of citizen journalists' reporting.

viii) Messaging and Communication Apps: Messaging and communication apps such as WhatsApp Signal or Telegram are invaluable for citizen journalists to communicate securely with sources, editors and fellow journalists. These apps offer end-to-end encryption, ensuring the privacy and security of conversations.

14. How to Report as a Citizen Journalist

As a citizen journalist, it is pivotal to understand the ethical responsibilities, standards and best practices to ensure accurate, reliable and impactful reporting.

i) Verify Information: One of the primary responsibilities of a citizen journalist is to verify the accuracy of the information they gather before reporting it. This involves fact-checking, cross-referencing multiple sources and seeking official statements or reliable witnesses. It is paramount to ensure that the information is credible, objective and free from personal biases. Verifying information helps maintain the integrity of the news and fosters trust among the audience.

ii) Be Objective and Impartial: Maintaining objectivity and impartiality is essential in citizen journalism. Reporters should present information without personal opinions or biases, allowing the audience to form their own judgments. Objectivity can be achieved by focusing on the facts, providing multiple perspectives and giving voice to diverse viewpoints. By presenting a balanced view, citizen journalists can enrich the trustworthiness of their reporting and avoid spreading misinformation.

iii) Respect Privacy and Consent: Respecting the privacy and consent of individuals who are part of the story is crucial. Citizen journalists should obtain informed consent before photographing, interviewing or filming individuals. It is important to be mindful of sensitive information, personal details and the potential impact on the privacy and safety of those involved. Respecting privacy and obtaining consent demonstrates ethical reporting practices and protects the rights of individuals.

iv) Use Ethical Visual Storytelling: Visual elements play a relevant role in citizen journalism. When capturing and sharing photos or videos, it is important to consider ethical guidelines. Avoid altering or manipulating visual content that could mislead or distort the truth. Captions and descriptions should accurately represent the context of the visuals. Balancing the power of visual storytelling with ethical considerations helps maintain the integrity of the news and prevents the spread of misleading information.

v) Engage in Responsible Social Media Use: Social media platforms are powerful tools for citizen journalists to circulate news content. However, responsible use is essential. Ensure that information shared on social media is accurate and reliable. Provide cite sources, context and avoid sensationalizing or exaggerating facts. Moreover, engage with the audience responsibly, encourage constructive dialogues and address any misinformation promptly. By being responsible social media users, citizen journalists can foster a positive and informed online community.

vi) Collaborate and Seek Expertise: Collaboration with other citizen journalists, professional journalists and subject matter experts can enhance the quality and impact of reporting. Seek feedback, guidance and insights from experienced journalists or experts in relevant fields. Collaborative efforts can lead to more comprehensive, accurate and nuanced reporting. Engaging with a network of fellow citizen journalists can also offer support, mentorship and opportunities for collective learning.

vii) Ensure Safety and Security: Safety is of utmost importance for citizen journalists. Prioritize personal safety and take necessary precautions while reporting in potentially risky or dangerous situations. Be aware of local laws and regulations regarding journalism. Protect the identities of sources or individuals who may face repercussions. Consider digital security by using secure communication tools, protecting personal data and being cautious of online threats. Reporting safely and securely allows citizen journalists to stay with their vital work without compromising their well-being.

viii) Reflect and Learn: Continuous learning and self-reflection are essential for growth as a citizen journalist. Reflect on your reporting practices, seek feedback and learn from any mistakes or challenges. Stay updated on media ethics, emerging trends and technological advancements that can enhance your reporting skills.

CHAPTER 2

CITIZEN JOURNALISM: STRENGTHS AND BENEFITS

One of the perks of citizen journalism is the diversity of perspectives it puts forth. Professional journalists most of the time work within the constraints of their news organizations, which may have their own biases or agendas. Citizen journalists, on the other hand, can arise from a wide range of backgrounds and experiences, and are frequently documenting issues that mainstream media may overlook. This can lead to a more comprehensive and nuanced understanding of events and issues.

Citizen journalism is the speed with which information can be disseminated. In a world where news cycles are constantly accelerating, citizen journalists are the first to report breaking news, providing crucial information in real-time. This can be especially important in situations where professional journalists may not have access, such as in areas of conflict or natural disasters.

Citizen journalism can give a voice to marginalized communities. In many cases, mainstream media outlets may not prioritize reporting on issues that affect minority groups, whereas citizen journalists from these communities may be more likely to cover such issues. This can help raise awareness of important issues and amplify the voices of those who are time and again ignored by the mainstream media.

1. Advantages of Citizen Journalism

There are several advantages of citizen journalism; they are increased diversity in news coverage, greater transparency and accountability and improved civic engagement.

One of the primary advantages of citizen journalism is the augmented diversity of news coverage. Traditional media outlets frequently rely on a small group of journalists to report on news and events, which can result in a narrow range of perspectives being presented. In contrast, citizen journalists come from a variety of backgrounds and have diverse interests and experiences. This multiplicity can lead to a broader range of stories being covered and a greater variety of sides being presented.

Citizen journalism also promotes transparency and accountability. In many cases, traditional media outlets are owned by large corporations or are subject to government regulation. This can create a conflict of interest or result in certain stories being suppressed. Citizen journalists are usually independent and not beholden to any specific agenda or interest. This independence can lead to a more obvious and frank representation of news and events.

Citizen journalism promotes civic engagement. As citizens become more involved in collecting and reporting news, they become more engaged with their communities and the issues that affect them. This can lead to increased awareness of important issues and a greater sense of civic responsibility. They can provide a platform for underrepresented communities to voice their concerns and be heard.

Citizen journalism also has the potential to promote social change. By reporting on stories that traditional media outlets might oversee or ignore, citizen journalists can bring attention to central matters and raise awareness among the public.

2. Transparency and Accountability

Transparency and accountability are two key principles that underpin the practice of citizen journalism. Citizen journalists, who are generally independent and not affiliated with traditional media outlets, have the ability to provide an exclusive perspective on news and events. However, this also places a substantial responsibility on them to ensure that their reporting is accurate, unbiased and accountable.

Transparency refers to the openness and honesty which citizen journalists uphold while reporting. This consists of being transparent about their sources, their methods of gathering information and their own biases or perspectives. By being transparent, citizen journalists can build trust with their audiences and ensure that their reporting is seen as credible and reliable.

One of the ways in which citizen journalists can promote transparency is through the use of open-source reporting tools. These tools allow citizen journalists to collaborate with each other and with their audiences to collect, verify and disseminate information. This can help make sure that their reporting is accurate, and that their sources are trustworthy.

Another essential feature of transparency is the willingness to correct mistakes and clarify information. Citizen journalists are mostly working under tight deadlines and without the resources available to traditional media outlets. This can lead to errors or inaccuracies in their reporting. However, by being transparent about these mistakes and correcting them promptly, citizen journalists can maintain their credibility and build trust with their audiences.

Accountability refers to the responsibility that citizen journalists have to ensure that their reporting is accurate, unbiased and fair. This includes being liable to their sources, audiences and the wider community.

Citizen journalists can promote accountability by adhering to a code of ethics. Many professional journalists adhere to a code of ethics that sets out standards for accuracy, fairness and impartiality. Citizen journalists can also adopt similar codes of ethics to guide their reporting and guarantee that they are abide to best practices.

Accountability accept feedback and criticism. Citizen journalists are many a time reporting on controversial or sensitive topics, and their reporting may be subject to scrutiny or criticism. Nevertheless, by being open to feedback and criticism, citizen journalists can improve their reporting and build trust with their audiences.

By being transparent about their sources, methods, biases and by being accountable for the accuracy, fairness and impartiality of their reporting, citizen journalists can build trust with their audiences and promote a more diverse and engaged media landscape. While there are challenges and risks associated with citizen journalism - accuracy and bias concerns - transparency and accountability can help mitigate these risks and safeguard that citizen journalism remains a valuable and important aspect of the modern media landscape.

3. Citizen Journalism and Society

Citizen journalism has become a prominent and transformative force in modern society. Enabled by digital technology and the rise of social media platforms, ordinary individuals now have the means to act as reporters, capturing and disseminating news and information from their unique standpoints. This phenomenon has had profound implications for society, influencing the media landscape, public discourse and democratic processes.

Traditional media outlets, with their gatekeeping role, have been supplemented by citizen journalists who can report on events and issues that may be disregarded by mainstream media. This has led to a more diverse range of perspectives being represented, giving voice to marginalized communities and bringing attention to local, grassroots stories that repeatedly go unobserved.

Citizen journalism has acted as a catalyst in disseminating news. With the widespread use of smartphones, individuals can instantly capture and share happenings as they unfold, often providing real-time updates on breaking news. This rapid spreading of information has proven priceless during emergencies and crises, allowing people to stay informed and make critical decisions. It has also fostered a greater sense of social activism and awareness. As individuals document and share stories related to social issues, injustices and human rights violations, they contribute to raising public consciousness and mobilizing collective action. Social media platforms have become powerful tools for organizing and amplifying advocacy efforts, ultimately leading to social and political change.

Citizen journalism is a potent force for societal change and empowerment. It has brought about a more engaged and participatory form of media consumption, where individuals are not passive consumers but active contributors to the public discourse. Through citizen journalism, people have a direct hand in shaping the narratives that define their communities and their lives, transcending geographical and cultural boundaries.

Citizen journalism's impact on society is not limited to news distribution and social activism; it also extends to shaping political discourse and influencing public opinion. With the rise of citizen journalists, political discussions have become more inclusive as ordinary individuals share their angles on political events and policy issues. This increased engagement has reinvigorated democratic processes by fostering greater citizen participation.

Social media platforms, in particular, have become a battleground for political discourse where citizens express their opinions, challenge prevailing narratives and hold politicians and policymakers accountable. The direct communication between citizens and political figures on these platforms has disrupted traditional communication channels and forced politicians to be more responsive to the concerns of their constituents.

Most importantly, Citizen journalism has played a momentous role in revealing corruption and exposing abuses of power. When traditional media outlets might be hesitant to confront powerful figures, citizen journalists are usually more willing to take risks and investigate matters that affect their communities directly. Their efforts have led to increased transparency and scrutiny of public officials and institutions, contributing to greater accountability in governance.

4. Impact of Citizen Journalism

One of the most significant impacts of citizen journalism has been on the coverage of breaking news. Citizen journalists are often the first to cover events as they happen, using social media and other online platforms to share photos videos and eyewitness accounts. This has enabled news organizations to quickly and accurately cover breaking news, providing up-to-the-minute coverage to audiences around the world.

Citizen journalism has also had an impact on the diversity of voices represented in the media. Traditional news organizations have been criticized for their lack of diversity, particularly in terms of race, gender and socioeconomic background. Citizen journalists are regularly more diverse than traditional journalists, and they bring a wider range of perspectives and experiences to the table.

Citizen journalism has been on the relationship between journalists and the public. In the past, journalists were seen as distant and disconnected from their audience. Moreover, it has assisted in breaking down these barriers, creating a more open and collaborative relationship between journalists and the public. Citizen journalists commonly work alongside professional journalists, sharing information and collaborating on stories. This has helped to build trust between journalists and the public, and has created a more engaged and informed citizenry.

Citizen journalism has also had an impact on the accountability of those in power. Citizen journalists are mostly the ones who disclose stories of corruption, abuse of power, and other wrongdoing. By shining a light on these issues, they have helped hold those in power accountable for their actions. This has had a substantial result on society, helping to ensure that those in power are held to a higher standard of accountability and transparency.

5. The Role of Citizen Journalism in Shaping Public Opinion

Citizen journalism plays a significant role in shaping public opinion, particularly in today's digital age where information is readily accessible and shared widely. It brings forth a wide range of perspectives that may not be represented in traditional media. Ordinary individuals, with their varied backgrounds, experiences, and beliefs, contribute to a more inclusive and diverse media landscape. This diversity of voices challenges dominant narratives and offers alternative viewpoints, allowing the public to consider a broader spectrum of opinions and form a more nuanced understanding of complex issues.

Citizen journalists focus on local or community-specific stories that may be overlooked by mainstream media outlets. By shedding light on these underreported or marginalized issues, Citizen journalism handles a prominent role in shaping public opinion by providing diverse outlooks, responding rapidly to breaking news, leveraging social media platforms and exposing injustices. While citizen journalism has the potential to foster an informed and engaged citizenry, individuals must remain vigilant in evaluating the credibility and accuracy of the information they consume, ensuring that public opinion is based on reliable and verified sources.

CHAPTER 3

CITIZEN JOURNALISM IN A GLOBAL CONTEXT

Citizen journalism has the potential to be a valuable addition to the world of journalism, providing a way for ordinary people to share their experiences and attitude on the world around them. In many parts of the world, citizen journalism has become a critical tool for holding governments and other powerful actors accountable. In countries with limited press freedom, citizen journalists may be the only ones able to report on human rights abuses, corruption and other issues. Though, this work can come at a great personal cost as citizen journalists may face censorship, harassment and even violence.

1. Abraham Zapruder

Abraham Zapruder, who filmed the assassination of American President John F Kennedy with a home-movie camera, is sometimes presented as an ancestor to citizen journalists.

Zapruder was a Ukrainian-born American clothing manufacturer who witnessed the assassination of John F. Kennedy in Texas, on November 22, 1963. He unexpectedly captured the shooting in a home movie while filming the presidential limousine and motor cade as it travelled through Dealey Plaza. The Zapruder film is regarded as the most complete footage of the assassination

As Kennedy's motorcade approached, Zapruder began filming the scene from his position on the north side of Elm Street, near the corner of Houston Street. He captured 26 seconds of footage that would become the most complete and vivid record of the assassination.

The footage was immediately recognized as a crucial piece of evidence in the investigation of the assassination. The FBI quickly seized the original film and made copies for use in the investigation. The Warren Commission, tasked with investigating the assassination, used the film extensively in their report, which concluded that Lee Harvey Oswald acted alone in shooting Kennedy.

The Zapruder film would go on to become one of the most studied and analysed pieces of film in history. It was repeatedly shown on television and in documentaries, becoming a powerful symbol of the assassination and the trauma it inflicted on the nation. The film also raised questions about the official version of events, with some researchers arguing that the film shows evidence of multiple shooters or a conspiracy.

Zapruder himself was thrust into the public eye and faced significant scrutiny and criticism for profiting off the film. He eventually sold the rights to Life magazine for $150,000, and the magazine published stills from the film in a special issue. Zapruder donated the original film to the National Archives, and it remains as one of the most important pieces of evidence in the history of American politics.

2. The 1988 U.S. Presidential Election

One of the earliest examples of citizen journalism occurred during the 1988 U.S. presidential election, where ordinary citizens played a pivotal role in shaping public opinion and influencing the outcome of the election.

During the 1988 U.S. presidential election, citizen journalists fulfilled a significant part in covering the campaign and reporting on the candidates' policies and positions. Notably, they were instrumental in exposing the weaknesses and scandals of the two main candidates, George H. W. Bush and Michael Dukakis. A group of citizen journalists uncovered the fact that Dukakis had vetoed a bill that would have required teachers to lead their classes in reciting the Pledge of Allegiance, a move that damaged his reputation with patriotic voters.

The citizen journalists showed their ability to report on events and issues that were not covered by mainstream media. They were able to provide in-depth coverage of local elections, which were habitually ignored by national news outlets. They also provided a venue for voices that were marginalised in the media, such as minority groups and activists, to share their perspectives and experiences with a wider audience.

They played a key role in fact-checking the claims made by the candidates and their supporters. They used their networks and expertise to verify information and expose falsehoods, which helped to promote greater transparency and accountability in the election process. This was particularly important given the prevalence of negative campaign ads and misleading rhetoric during the campaign. Through their reporting, fact-checking, and commentary, citizen journalists provided a valuable counterbalance to the mainstream media which helped to promote greater transparency and accountability in the election process.

3. The 1999 Seattle Protests

The 1999 Seattle protests, also known as the Battle of Seattle, were a series of demonstrations and civil unrest that took place during the World Trade Organization (WTO) Ministerial Conference in Seattle, Washington. The protests were largely organized by a coalition of labour unions, environmentalists and anti-globalization activists who were concerned about the impact of WTO policies on labour rights, environmental regulations and economic inequality. The protests received widespread coverage from mainstream media outlets, but they also marked a turning point in the development of citizen journalism as ordinary citizens used new media technologies to document and report on the protests from their own perspectives.

During the Seattle protests, citizen journalists used various forms of media including blogs, podcasts and videos to share their encounters and interpretations with a global audience. They captured images and footage of police brutality and excessive use of force, as well as the creative and artistic displays of protest that took place throughout the city. This allowed for a more refined and mixed portrayal of the protests, which contrasted with the more simplistic and often sensationalized coverage provided by mainstream media outlets.

In addition to providing alternative perspectives on the protests, citizen journalists also carried out a fundamental role in organizing and coordinating the demonstrations. They used online platforms to share information about protest routes, organize direct actions and provide medical and legal support for those who were arrested or injured. This helped create a more decentralized and democratic model of protest organizing which was less reliant on traditional hierarchical structures and more responsive to the needs and concerns of individual activists.

The role of citizen journalism in the Seattle protests helped highlight the power of new media technologies in enabling ordinary citizens to participate in the creation and dissemination of news and information.

4. 9/11 and Citizen Journalism

On September 11, 2001, the world was stunned by a series of terrorist attacks on the United States. Four commercial airplanes were hijacked by terrorists, with two of them flown into the twin towers of the World Trade Centre in New York City, one flown into the Pentagon in Washington D.C., and the fourth crashed in a field in Pennsylvania. These attacks resulted in the deaths of nearly 3,000 people and left a profound impact on the world.

The events of 9/11 were documented in real-time by both professional and amateur journalists. The rise of citizen journalism played a significant role in the coverage of the attacks, with many people capturing and sharing images and videos of the events as they unfolded.

During the 9/11, citizen journalists provided a unique perspective on the events that unfolded, capturing footage that was not available to professional journalists. These videos and images provided a raw, unfiltered look at the tragedy and helped shape the narrative of what happened on that fateful day.

One of the most iconic images from 9/11 was captured by citizen journalist Mark LaGanga. LaGanga was a producer for CBS News at the time and was on his way to work when the first plane hit the North Tower. He immediately began filming the scene, capturing footage of the towers as they burned and eventually collapsed. LaGanga's footage was later used by CBS News and other media outlets to provide a first-hand account of the events of that day.

Another notable example of citizen journalism during 9/11 was the work of Rick Rescorla. Rescorla was a security officer at the World Trade Centre and was responsible for evacuating employees from the towers during the attack. He was also a decorated veteran who had served in the Vietnam War and had trained his colleagues on how to respond to a terrorist attack. Rescorla's efforts saved countless lives, and his story was later shared in news reports and documentaries about the attacks.

The rise of citizen journalism during 9/11 was a significant moment in the history of media. It demonstrated the power of ordinary people to capture and share news content, and it provided a unique perspective on the events of that day. The proliferation of social media platforms in the years since 9/11 has only further expanded the reach of citizen journalism, making it easier than ever for people to share news content with a global audience.

5. The 2004 Tsunami and Citizen Journalism

On December 26, 2004, a devastating earthquake and subsequent tsunami struck the Indian Ocean region, resulting in one of the deadliest natural disasters in modern history. The tsunami claimed the lives of over 230,000 people in fourteen different countries. In the aftermath of the disaster, citizen journalism played a crucial role in documenting the tragedy and sharing information with the world.

During the 2004 tsunami, many people were able to document the disaster through photographs and videos, providing a unique and heart-breaking perspective on the devastation.

One of the most well-known examples of citizen journalism during the 2004 tsunami was the work of Swedish journalist, Magnus Holmgren. Holmgren was vacationing in Thailand with his family when the tsunami struck. He immediately began capturing footage of the disaster on his video camera, documenting the chaos and devastation as it unfolded. Holmgren's footage was later used by news organizations around the world and helped raise awareness of the scale of the disaster.

Another example was the work of a group of bloggers known as the Tsunami Help Blog. The blog was created as a way to share information about the disaster and provide updates on relief efforts. The blog quickly became a central hub for gathering data about the disaster, with contributions from people all over the world. The blog helped connect people who were looking for information about loved ones and provided a way for people to donate money and resources to those affected by the disaster.

The rise of citizen journalism during the 2004 tsunami had a meaningful impact on the way that the world understood the disaster. Through social media and online platforms, ordinary people were able to share their stories and document the tragedy in a way that was not possible through traditional media channels. This type of reporting helped humanize the disaster, giving a voice to those who had been affected by the tragedy.

6. The 2010 Haiti Earthquake

The 2010 Haiti earthquake was a catastrophic disaster that resulted in the loss of thousands of lives, widespread destruction and displacement of millions of people. The earthquake also marked a turning point in the development of citizen journalism as ordinary citizens used social media and other digital platforms to document and report on the disaster from their own perspectives.

In the immediate aftermath of the earthquake, citizen journalists used social media platforms such as Twitter and Facebook to share real-time updates on the situation in Haiti. They shared details about the extent of the damage, the number of casualties, and the efforts to provide aid and support to those affected by the disaster. These updates provided a valuable source of information for people around the world who were concerned about the situation in Haiti and wanted to stay informed about the ongoing relief efforts.

Citizen journalists were also able to use their networks and knowledge of local communities to provide more detailed and nuanced coverage of the earthquake. They shared stories of individual experiences, highlighted the impact of the disaster on marginalized communities, and reported on the challenges and successes of relief efforts. This helped provide a more comprehensive and diverse perspective on the disaster, which contrasted with the more limited coverage provided by mainstream media outlets.

In addition to providing information and coverage, citizen journalists also served a key role in mobilizing support for relief efforts. They used their social media platforms to share links to donation pages and fundraising initiatives, as well as to provide information about how people could get involved and support the ongoing efforts in Haiti. This helped create a more decentralized and participatory model of disaster response, which was less reliant on traditional aid organizations and more responsive to the needs and concerns of individual citizens.

7. The Arab Spring

The Arab Spring was a series of pro-democracy uprisings and demonstrations that swept across several countries in the Middle East and North Africa (MENA) region, starting in late 2010 and continuing into 2011 and beyond. The movement was characterized by widespread public discontent, demands for political reforms, economic opportunities and an end to authoritarian rule in the region.

The spark that ignited the Arab Spring was the self-immolation of Mohamed Bouazizi, a young Tunisian street vendor, in December 2010. His desperate act of protest against government corruption and mistreatment by authorities resonated with many

Tunisians and sparked protests against President Zine El Abidine Ben Ali's oppressive regime. After weeks of demonstrations and civil disobedience, Ben Ali fled to Saudi Arabia in January 2011, marking the first successful ouster of an Arab leader in the movement.

Inspired by the events in Tunisia, protests erupted in several other Arab countries, including Egypt, Libya, Yemen, Syria, Bahrain, and others. Each country had its unique political and social dynamics but the underlying causes were similar: frustration with autocratic rule, economic hardships, high unemployment rates, government corruption and a lack of political freedoms and civil liberties.

The Arab Spring led to significant political changes in some countries while facing violence, repression, and a return to authoritarianism in others:

Egypt: In February 2011, massive protests led to the resignation of long-time President Hosni Mubarak, who had ruled the country for nearly three decades. But, the transition to democracy was challenging, and Egypt's first democratically elected president, Mohamed Morsi, was ousted in a military coup in 2013, leading to a subsequent return to authoritarian rule under President Abdel Fattah el-Sisi.

Libya: The Libyan protests escalated into a full-fledged civil war, leading to the overthrow and death of Colonel Muammar Gaddafi in October 2011. However, Libya descended into chaos and political fragmentation with various factions vying for power and control over the country.

Yemen: Protests in Yemen led to President Ali Abdullah Saleh stepping down in February 2012. The country faced political instability, ongoing violence and the rise of extremist groups, exacerbating the humanitarian crisis.

Syria: Protests in Syria quickly turned into a brutal and protracted civil war after President Bashar al-Assad's regime responded with a violent crackdown. The conflict has resulted in widespread devastation, loss of life and a massive refugee crisis.

Bahrain: The government cracked down on protests in Bahrain, with the assistance of Saudi Arabia, leading to ongoing political repression and human rights abuses.

While the Arab Spring led to major political changes and offered hope for democratic reform, the outcomes varied greatly across the region. Some countries experienced genuine political transformations, while others witnessed repression and a return to authoritarianism. The aftermath of the Arab Spring continues to shape the political, social and economic landscape of the MENA region, with ongoing struggles for democracy, human rights and stability.

Social media occupies an instrumental role in the Arab Spring, serving as a powerful tool for communication, organization and mobilization of protesters. It facilitated the rapid spread of information and allowed activists to connect, coordinate and share their grievances with a global audience. Here are some ways in which social media impacted the Arab Spring:

i) Information Dissemination: Social media platforms, particularly Twitter, Facebook, and YouTube, became the primary sources of real-time information during the uprisings. Activists used these platforms to share news, videos and images of protests, government crackdowns and human rights abuses. This rapid dissemination of information countered government censorship and allowed the world to witness the events as they unfolded.

ii) Mobilization and Organization: Social media provided a decentralized and accessible platform for activists to organize and coordinate protests and demonstrations. Hashtags and online campaigns helped rally supporters, attract international attention and amplify the messages of the movements. This level of connectivity and accessibility was unprecedented and enabled the rapid mobilization of large numbers of people.

iii) International Solidarity: Social media allowed activists and supporters worldwide to express solidarity with the protesters. The use of common hashtags and sharing of images and messages helped create a sense of global connectedness and support for the demands of the protesters.

iv) Evading Government Censorship: Social media provided a platform for protesters to communicate and organize outside of traditional government-controlled media channels. Governments many a time tried to censor or shut down social media platforms during the uprisings, but activists found ways to circumvent these restrictions, such as using virtual private networks (VPNs) or other encrypted communication tools.

v) Instant Visibility: The viral nature of social media allowed events in one country to quickly capture the attention of the global community. This visibility puts pressure on governments and international actors to respond to the unfolding crises and the demands of the protesters.

vi) Challenges and Misinformation: While social media was a powerful tool for activism, it also presented challenges. Misinformation and rumours could spread rapidly, leading to confusion and potential harm. Additionally, the anonymity of social media allowed some actors to manipulate narratives and spread propaganda, both in support of and against the protesters.

Social media played a pivotal role in the Arab Spring by empowering protesters with the ability to organize, communicate and distribute information in real time. It became a double-edged sword, providing a platform for activism and mobilization, while also presenting challenges related to misinformation and government surveillance. The Arab Spring demonstrated the immense impact of social media in shaping political movements and how digital communication tools have become integral to modern-day protests and revolutions.

8. The Occupy Wall Street Movement

The Occupy Wall Street movement was a global protest movement that emerged in September 2011, in response to growing economic inequality and the perceived influence of wealthy elites on the political process. The movement began as a small group of protesters in New York City's Zuccotti Park, but quickly spread to other cities across the United States and around the world.

During the Occupy Wall Street protests, citizen journalists undertook a pivotal role in documenting and reporting on the movement from a grassroots perspective. They used social media platforms such as Twitter and Facebook to share real-time updates on the protests, including images and videos of police brutality, peaceful demonstrations and creative displays of protest. They also used online platforms to coordinate direct actions, share information about protest routes and provide medical and legal support for those who were arrested or injured.

In addition to providing alternative perspectives on the Occupy Wall Street movement, citizen journalists also helped shape the public discourse surrounding the movement. They provided a platform for voices that were frequently excluded from mainstream media coverage, including the perspectives of marginalized communities and working-class individuals. This helped create a more diverse and inclusive narrative about the movement, which was less focused on the more sensationalistic aspects of the protests and more on the underlying social and economic issues that the movement sought to address.

9. The 2013 Protests in Turkey

In 2013, Turkey experienced a wave of protests that were sparked by the government's plans to redevelop a park in central Istanbul. What began as a small environmental protest quickly grew into a larger movement against the ruling Justice and Development Party (AKP), which was accused of increasingly authoritarian and repressive tactics.

The protests were largely organized through social media platforms, with citizens using Twitter and other digital tools to coordinate demonstrations and share information about police brutality and government repression. The use of social media allowed for a decentralized and fluid movement that was able to quickly adapt to changing circumstances and respond to emerging threats.

The protests were marked by a diverse range of participants, including young people, students and members of various political and social groups. Protesters were united by a shared desire to challenge the government's increasingly authoritarian tactics, as well as to demand greater transparency and accountability in the political process.

One of the defining features of the protests was the use of creative and artistic displays of protest. Protesters used music, dance, and other forms of public art to express their dissent and to draw attention to the underlying social and political issues driving the movement. This helped create a more diverse and inclusive narrative about the protests, which was less focused on the more sensationalistic aspects of the demonstrations and more on the broader social and political concerns driving the movement.

The government's response to the protests was widely criticized for its heavy-handed tactics and use of violence against peaceful demonstrators. Police used tear gas, water cannons, and rubber bullets to disperse crowds, and protesters were regularly subjected to arbitrary arrests and detentions. The government's response only served to further fuel the protests and to galvanize public support for the movement.

While the protests ultimately did not achieve many of their policy goals, they succeeded in creating a broad-based social movement that challenged the government's authoritarian tactics and demanded greater transparency and accountability in the political process. It also demonstrated the power of citizen activism and creative protest in challenging entrenched political systems and promoting greater social and political change.

Notable for the role played by citizen journalists in documenting and sharing information about the protests from a grassroots perspective. As traditional media outlets were largely censored or silenced by the government, citizen journalists stepped in to provide real-time updates on the protests and to share images and videos of police brutality and government repression.

Social media platforms such as Twitter and Facebook performed a central role in enabling citizen journalists to report on the protests and to mobilize public support for the movement. These platforms allowed for the rapid dissemination of information and helped create a sense of solidarity and shared purpose among the diverse range of protesters who participated in the demonstrations.

10. The Black Lives Matter Movement

The Black Lives Matter movement is a social justice movement that emerged in response to the ongoing police brutality and systemic racism faced by Black people in the United States. The movement began in 2013, following the acquittal of George Zimmerman in the killing of Trayvon Martin, and gained substantial momentum in 2014, following the deaths of Michael Brown and Eric Garner at the hands of police officers.

Black Lives Matter movement has been the role played by citizen journalists in documenting and sharing information about police violence and government repression. As traditional media outlets have many times failed to adequately cover issues of police violence and systemic racism, citizen journalists have stepped in to provide real-time updates on incidents of police brutality and to share images and videos of the human rights abuses committed against Black people.

Social media platforms such as Twitter, Facebook and Instagram have played a critical role in enabling citizen journalists to report on the movement and to mobilize public support for the victims of police violence. These platforms have allowed for the rapid spreading of information and helped to create a sense of solidarity and shared purpose among the diverse range of people affected by systemic racism.

Citizen journalists have also played a critical role in countering government propaganda and misinformation about the movement. They have used social media to share accurate information about the movement and to debunk false claims made by the police and other government officials. This has helped create a more nuanced and accurate understanding of the movement and to counter the government's efforts to suppress dissent and stifle frees speech.

11. The Murder of George Floyd

The murder of George Floyd in May 2020 served as a poignant example of the impact of citizen journalism in exposing systemic issues and promoting social justice. The incident, captured on video by a bystander, illustrated the role that citizen journalism can play in shedding light on instances of police brutality and sparking a global movement for racial justice.

The video, recorded by Darnella Frazier, a young individual who happened to be present at the scene, depicted the harrowing moments of George Floyd, an unarmed Black man, being restrained by police officer Derek Chauvin, who knelt on Floyd's neck for an extended period. Frazier's footage quickly spread across social media platforms, generating outrage, protests and calls for justice.

The significance of citizen journalism in this case cannot be overstated. Frazier's video provided vital visual evidence that challenged the initial police narrative, which sought to downplay the severity of the incident. The video captured Floyd's desperate pleas for help and his struggles to breathe, creating a visceral impact on viewers worldwide. It prompted widespread scrutiny of police practices, systemic racism and the urgent need for reform. The video served as a catalyst for citizen-led activism and grassroots organizing. Social media platforms became powerful tools for circulating information, mobilizing protests and amplifying demands for justice. Hashtags such as #JusticeForGeorgeFloyd and #BlackLivesMatter spread rapidly, allowing individuals to contribute their voices, share personal experiences and offer diverse perspectives on the issue.

Citizen journalists and activists utilized social media to share real-time updates, livestream protests, document instances of police aggression and provide educational resources for advocacy. These efforts helped the movement gain momentum, attract global attention, and transcend geographical boundaries. Citizen journalism played a salient part in driving the narrative, offering alternative perspectives, and highlighting stories that traditional media might have overlooked or underreported.

The impact of citizen journalism in the murder of George Floyd extended beyond immediate awareness and protests. It spurred public pressure, leading to the arrest and subsequent trial of Derek Chauvin. The video evidence presented during the trial played a pivotal role in holding Chauvin accountable for his actions. The case exemplified how citizen journalism can influence legal proceedings and contribute to ensuring justice is served.

12. The Role of Chinese Citizen Journalists During the COVID-19 Pandemic

The COVID-19 pandemic has underscored the importance of reliable information and the critical role that citizen journalism plays in shaping public awareness and response. In China, where the outbreak first emerged, citizen journalists emerged as a powerful force in transmitting news and shedding light on the situation.

Chinese citizen journalism gained prominence during the early stages of the pandemic, as traditional media faced limitations in reporting on the evolving situation. Citizen journalists, armed with smartphones and social media platforms, became the eyes and ears of the public. They captured and shared firsthand accounts, videos and testimonies, offering an unfiltered perspective that challenged official narratives.

One notable example is Zhang Zhan, a citizen journalist who documented the Wuhan lockdown and shared her experiences on social media platforms. Zhang Zhan gained international attention for her reporting on the COVID-19 situation in Wuhan. She documented the impact of the virus, the overwhelmed healthcare system, and the strict lockdown measures imposed by the Chinese government. Zhang's firsthand accounts and videos provided vital insights into the severity of the situation. However, she was arrested in May 2020 and later sentenced to four years in prison, becoming a symbol of the challenges faced by citizen journalists in China.

Chen Qiushi, a former lawyer, is another citizen journalist, who has travelled to Wuhan in the early stages of the outbreak. He documented the overwhelmed hospitals, interviewed patients and medical workers, and reported on the conditions in the epicentre of the virus. Chen's videos and social media updates drew attention to the severity of the crisis and helped raise awareness globally. But, he went missing in February 2020, and his whereabouts remain unknown.

Li Zehua, a former journalist for China Central Television (CCTV), gained attention for his independent reporting in Wuhan. After the disappearance of Chen Qiushi and Fang Bin, Li took it upon himself to continue their work. He filmed and live-streamed his experiences, investigating the local markets and hospitals. Li was briefly detained by authorities and subsequently released, but he chose to remain silent on the details of his detention.

These citizen journalists, among others, played a critical duty in bringing attention to the severity of the COVID-19 crisis in China and the challenges faced by the public. Their brave reporting and documentation provided alternative perspectives, challenged official narratives and helped shape global understanding of the pandemic. However, their work also exposed the risks faced by those who question the government's response, highlighting the challenges to independent journalism in China.

While Chinese citizen journalism demonstrated its power and resilience during the pandemic, it faced numerous challenges and limitations. Government censorship and surveillance remained significant hurdles, with citizen journalists subjected to intimidation, harassment and even arrest. The absence of legal protections for independent journalism restricted their ability to operate freely and independently.

CHAPTER 4

CITIZEN JOURNALISM AND INDIA

The history of citizen journalism in India can be traced back to the country's independence movement, a point where newspapers played a crucial role in spreading information and mobilizing the masses. However, it wasn't until the advent of the internet and digital media in the late 1990s that citizen journalism began to truly take hold in India.

The first wave of citizen journalism in India was driven by bloggers who used online platforms to share their opinions and perspectives on various issues. One of the most notable examples of this was the Indian Blogosphere, which emerged in the mid-2000s and included a diverse range of bloggers covering everything from politics and current affairs to culture and entertainment.

Another significant development in the history of citizen journalism in India was the rise of hyperlocal news websites and community-driven platforms. In the early 2010s, a number of websites like *Citizen Matters* and *The Better India* emerged, which focused on providing news and information about specific neighbourhoods or communities. These websites were often run by volunteers and relied on citizen contributions to create their content.

Social media platforms like Twitter and Facebook also played a significant role in the growth of citizen journalism in India. During the Arab Spring in 2011, social media was widely used to spread information and organise protests, and this trend was quickly picked up by Indian activists and citizen journalists. In 2013, the Indian government blocked access to several social media platforms in response to communal violence in the state of Assam, leading to widespread criticism and calls for greater freedom of expression.

In recent years, citizen journalism in India has become increasingly professionalized, with a number of independent news outlets and media startups emerging to fill gaps in the traditional media landscape. These outlets, such as The Wire and Scroll.in, usually focus on investigative journalism and critical analysis of political and social issues, and have become an important source of information for many Indians.

Citizen journalism has become a powerful force in India, shaping the country's media landscape and providing an alternative perspective on the issues that matter most. From bloggers and hyperlocal news websites to independent media outlets and startups, citizen journalists have emerged as an pivotal source of information and analysis in a country with a long history of government control over the media.

1. The 2008 Mumbai Terror Attack

In November 2008, a series of coordinated terrorist attacks hit Mumbai, India, killing over 160 people and injuring hundreds more. During the attacks, citizen journalism played a crucial role in reporting on the unfolding events and providing updates on the situation.

One example of citizen journalism during the Mumbai attacks was the work of Vinu, a blogger who lived in Mumbai. Vinu began documenting the events on his blog as soon as news of the attacks broke, providing updates on the locations of the attacks and the number of casualties. He also shared photographs and videos taken by himself and other witnesses, helping to paint a vivid picture of the chaos and destruction that was taking place.

Another example was the work of several Twitter users who were on the ground in Mumbai. These users were able to provide real-time updates on the situation, sharing information about the locations of the attacks and the movements of the attackers. One

Twitter user, who went by the handle @livefist, provided updates on the situation at the Taj Hotel where hostages were being held by the attackers. His tweets were picked up by news organizations around the world, helping to keep people informed about the situation as it unfolded.

The rise of citizen journalism during the Mumbai attacks had a significant impact on the way that the world understood the situation. Through social media and online platforms, ordinary people were able to share their stories and document the tragedy in a way that was not possible through traditional media channels. This type of reporting helped humanize the attacks, giving a voice to those who had been affected by the tragedy.

2. The 2012 Delhi Gang Rape

The 2012 Delhi Gang Rape was a horrific incident that occurred in India in which a 23-year-old woman was brutally gang-raped and assaulted by six men on a moving bus. The incident sparked outrage across India and around the world, with people calling for justice for the victim and demanding changes to India's laws and attitudes towards sexual violence.

Citizen journalism played an important role in the aftermath of the incident, Citizen Journalists, both in India and around the world, helped raise awareness about the incident and put pressure on the Indian government to take action.

The mainstream media was criticized for their lack of coverage and insensitivity towards the victim. But, social media played a vital role in bringing the case to the forefront of public attention. Citizens used Twitter, Facebook, and other social media platforms to express their outrage and demand justice for the victim. The coverage by citizen journalists eventually led to nationwide protests and a change in the country's laws on sexual assault.

The use of social media by citizen journalists helped bring attention to the issue of sexual violence in India and to highlight the inadequacy of the country's legal system in addressing these crimes. Citizen journalists shared stories and personal experiences of sexual violence and helped to create a groundswell of public opinion in support of the victim and her family.

The incident also led to the creation of new online platforms and initiatives focused on supporting victims of sexual violence, such as the website "Safe City", which allows people to report incidents of sexual harassment and violence in public spaces. The incident also helped spur changes to India's legal system, including the introduction of tougher penalties for rape and the creation of fast-track courts to hear sexual assault cases.

3. The Anna Hazare Movement

In 2011, the anti-corruption movement led by social activist Anna Hazare took India by storm, with thousands of people joining the movement in support of a strong Lokpal Bill. Citizen journalism played a crucial role in reporting on the movement and bringing attention to the issue of corruption in India.

Anna Hazare is an Indian social activist who became the face of the anti-corruption movement in India in 2011. The main reason behind the protest was the rampant corruption in India, which had become a major issue affecting the country's economy and development.

The movement led by Anna Hazare was aimed at pressuring the Indian government to enact a strong anti-corruption law known as the Lokpal Bill. The bill sought to establish an independent ombudsman to investigate and prosecute cases of corruption involving public officials, including the Prime Minister of India.

The anti-corruption movement led by Anna Hazare gained widespread support across India, with thousands of people joining the protests in major cities across the country. The protesters argued that corruption was a major obstacle to the development and progress of India and that the government needed to take urgent action to address the issue.

The movement was also fuelled by a growing sense of frustration among ordinary citizens who felt that corruption had become endemic in Indian society, with public officials routinely engaging in corrupt practices and getting away with it. The protesters demanded that the Lokpal Bill be passed into law as soon as possible, in order to bring an end to the culture of corruption in India.

Despite facing opposition from some quarters, the movement was successful in raising awareness about the issue of corruption in India and forcing the government to take action. In 2013, the Lokpal Bill was finally passed by the Indian parliament, marking a significant victory for the anti-corruption movement and the people of India.

4. CGNet Swara

There are numerous initiatives taken up by citizen journalists in their communities. The story of Shubhranshu Choudhary and the 'Voice of Chhattisgarh' is an example. Choudhary is a former BBC journalist and founder of CGNet

Swara – a democratic tool of India. It is a system developed with the help of Microsoft Research India to allow people to use mobile phones to send and listen to audio reports in their local language.

Choudhary has created a boom in the tribal land of Chhattisgarh by creating a technology to help and increase global reach by virtue of its websites and training professional journalists at the same time. CGNet Swara is transforming the shape of India in terms of communicating, sharing and receiving news.

He spoke with the indigenous Gondi people and heard about their difficulties – lack of schools, broken infrastructure, and corruption.

The platform uses a combination of mobile phones and the internet to allow people in remote and rural areas to share their stories and concerns. It works on a "missed call" system, where citizens can give a missed call to a toll-free number to report news or issues in their area. The reports are then verified by a team of moderators before being shared with the wider community.

CGNet Swara has been instrumental in amplifying the voices of marginalized and tribal communities in India. It has helped bring attention to issues such as land rights, forest conservation, and government schemes, which are frequently ignored by mainstream media outlets.

The platform has also been used to report on incidents of violence, discrimination, and human rights abuses against marginalized communities. Citizen journalists have reported on cases of police brutality, caste-based violence, and discrimination against women and girls.

CGNet Swara has been successful in bringing attention to these issues and driving change at the local and national levels. The platform has been used to mobilize support and resources for marginalized communities and has also been instrumental in holding government officials and public institutions accountable for their actions.

Over the years, tribal India has benefited because of citizen journalism in several ways. This is one part of India which desperately seeks a hand for help and needs to voice itself. Hence, citizen journalism finds its way as an alternative outlet to help tribals raise their voice against the local problems and disparities that they find hard to talk about otherwise.

5. The 2015 Chennai Floods

The Chennai floods of 2015 were a devastating natural disaster that struck the Indian city of Chennai and the surrounding areas in November and December of that year. The floods were caused by heavy rainfall and resulted in considerable damage to property, infrastructure, and loss of life.

The Chennai floods of 2015 were the result of the heaviest rainfall the city had experienced in over a century. The city's drainage systems were unable to cope with the amount of water, causing floods in many areas. In addition, several lakes and reservoirs in the region were already at capacity due to the earlier monsoon season, exacerbating the flood situation.

The floods had a notable impact on the city of Chennai, with thousands of people being displaced from their homes and many areas of the city being cut off due to the flooding. The disaster also had a significant impact on the region's infrastructure, with roads and bridges being washed away and public transport being severely disrupted.

Citizen journalism played an important role during the Chennai floods of 2015, with many people using social media platforms to report on the situation and share information about the relief efforts. Social media users shared photographs and videos of the floods, highlighting the extent of the damage and the impact on the local population.

The use of citizen journalism during the Chennai floods helped mobilize relief efforts and raise awareness about the situation. Many people used social media to coordinate rescue efforts and distribute relief supplies, helping to provide much-needed support to the affected communities.

6. The 2018 Kerala Floods

In 2018, the picturesque state of Kerala, known for its serene backwaters, lush landscapes, and vibrant culture, faced one of its most challenging periods in history. The monsoon season that year unleashed a devastating flood, leaving a trail of destruction and loss. The Kerala floods of 2018 were a stark reminder of the immense power of nature and the urgent need to adapt and respond to climate-related disasters.

During June, July, and August, Kerala typically experiences heavy rainfall as part of the annual monsoon. However, in 2018, the intensity and duration of the rain surpassed all expectations. The state witnessed an unprecedented deluge, with rainfall measuring well above the average levels for the season. The Kerala floods affected all 14 districts of the state, causing widespread devastation and displacement of communities. Rivers swelled to dangerous levels, overflowing their banks and submerging vast areas. Towns and villages were transformed into vast waterlogged landscapes, leaving people stranded and isolated.

The Kerala floods of 2018 brought to the forefront the critical role of social media in disaster management and response. During this calamity, social media platforms played a pivotal role in disseminating information, coordinating rescue efforts, and providing support to the affected communities. Some ways in which social media impacted the Kerala floods were:

i) Real-time Updates and Information Sharing: Social media platforms such as Twitter, Facebook, and WhatsApp became vital sources of real-time information during the floods. Residents, journalists, and citizen journalists used these platforms to share updates about the flood situation, weather conditions, and areas that needed immediate assistance. This enabled authorities and relief agencies to stay informed and respond promptly to the evolving crisis.

ii) Emergency Communication: With conventional communication infrastructure regularly disrupted during disasters, social media offered an alternative means of communication. People used Facebook's Safety Check feature to mark themselves safe, reassuring friends and family members about their well-being. WhatsApp groups were formed to exchange critical information and coordinate rescue operations.

iii) Request for Help and Volunteer Mobilization: Social media provided a platform for affected individuals to request help and for volunteers to offer their services. People used hashtags and geolocation tags to identify their locations and seek assistance. Volunteers and rescue teams used social media to organize their efforts, reaching out to those in distress and providing aid.

iv) Crowdsourced Rescue and Relief Operations: Citizen journalists and ordinary individuals became active participants in rescue and relief operations through social media. They shared information about people stranded in certain areas, and this data was used by rescue teams to direct their efforts efficiently. The power of crowdsourcing allowed for a wider reach and increased effectiveness in rescue missions.

v) Awareness and Fundraising: Social media played a significant role in raising awareness about the flood situation in Kerala. People from across the globe were able to witness the extent of the disaster through images and videos shared on social media. Additionally, crowdfunding campaigns were organized through platforms like GoFundMe, enabling people to donate funds to support relief efforts in Kerala.

vi) Spreading Safety Information: Social media platforms were used to share safety guidelines and instructions during the floods. Information about evacuation routes, emergency helpline numbers, and precautionary measures was widely circulated through various social media channels, helping people make informed decisions during the crisis.

vii) Providing Emotional Support: Social media became a space for emotional support and solidarity during difficult times. People shared messages of hope, empathy, and encouragement, providing comfort to those affected by the floods.

The Kerala floods of 2018 showcased the transformative power of social media in disaster management. These platforms facilitated communication, coordination, and support on a massive scale, enabling swift and effective responses to the crisis. Social media's role in the Kerala floods serves as a powerful reminder of its potential to be a force for good during emergencies, but it also underscores the importance of responsible usage and information verification in such situations.

7. The Aarey Forest Issue

The Aarey forest issue is a long-standing controversy in Mumbai, India, centred on the use of a 1,280-acre plot of land that is part of the larger Sanjay Gandhi National Park. The plot is home to a dense forest ecosystem that has been designated as a critical wildlife habitat by the government, with more than 5,000 trees on the site.

In recent years, the plot has been the subject of intense debate and controversy, with some groups advocating for its development for various infrastructure projects, while others have been calling for its preservation as a critical ecological zone.

The issue came to a head in 2019 when the Mumbai Metro Rail Corporation (MMRC) announced plans to clear a significant portion of the Aarey forest for the construction of a metro car shed. The plan sparked a massive outcry from environmental activists and citizens who argued that the destruction of the forest would have catastrophic consequences for the local ecosystem and exacerbate the already critical air pollution problem in Mumbai.

Citizen journalism played a significant role in bringing the issue to the forefront of public consciousness, with social media platforms being used to raise awareness about the issue and organize protests and demonstrations. Many people used social media to share photos and videos of the Aarey forest, highlighting the importance of preserving the area for future generations.

The public outcry eventually led to a court case, with the Bombay High Court issuing a stay order on the construction of the metro car shed in the Aarey forest. The court cited the importance of preserving the area's biodiversity and ecology, as well as the need to address the city's worsening air pollution problem.

The Aarey forest issue is a prime example of the power of citizen journalism in raising awareness about critical environmental issues and mobilizing public opinion to effect change. The public outcry and legal action demonstrate the necessity of preserving natural ecosystems and the need for responsible and sustainable urban planning practices.

8. India's COVID-19 Crisis

Citizen journalism has played a pivotal role in handling India's COVID-19 crisis, which has been one of the worst in the world. With a lack of accurate and reliable information from official sources, citizen journalists have stepped in to provide important updates, news, and analysis on the pandemic.

Citizen journalists have used various platforms like social media, blogs, and podcasts to provide real-time updates on the COVID-19 situation in different parts of the country. They have reported on the number of cases, deaths, and recoveries in their local communities and shared information on the availability of hospital beds, oxygen cylinders, and other critical resources.

Citizen journalists have also considerably influenced debunking myths and misinformation surrounding the pandemic. They have fact-checked information shared by politicians, celebrities, and other influential people, and provided accurate and reliable information to the public.

With the rapid spread of information and the need for up-to-date and accurate reporting, they became instrumental in dispersing vital health-related information, sharing personal experiences, and fostering community engagement.

During the pandemic, citizen journalists have the advantage of being on the ground in their communities. They can provide real-time reporting on local developments, including the availability of healthcare services, testing sites, and vaccination centres. This localized reporting is invaluable, as it helps individuals access critical information promptly and make informed decisions about their health and well-being.

Citizen journalists act as intermediaries, bridging the gap between expert knowledge and the general public. They distilled complex scientific information into accessible language, making it easier for individuals to understand public health guidelines, prevention strategies and the latest research. By translating scientific jargon into everyday language, citizen journalists empowered communities to make informed decisions and take appropriate actions to protect themselves and others.

Citizen journalism played a vital role in health communication during pandemics, ensuring that accurate and timely information reaches communities, promoting inclusive narratives, and countering misinformation. By amplifying diverse perspectives, bridging the gap between experts and the public, and engaging communities, citizen journalists empower individuals to make informed decisions and take necessary actions to protect their health. However, with this power comes the responsibility to report ethically, fact-check rigorously and prioritize the well-being of communities. By upholding these principles, citizen journalism becomes a valuable ally in public health efforts, fostering resilience, trust, and effective communication during challenging times.

9. The Public Sphere in India

Citizen journalism has become an increasingly important aspect of the public sphere in India, as people have become more empowered to share their views, opinions, and experiences through various media channels. The public sphere refers to the space where individuals can express their views and opinions freely, without fear of censorship or repression. It is an essential component of democracy as it allows citizens to participate in public debate and shape public policy.

In India, citizen journalism has played a decisive role in expanding the public sphere and promoting greater transparency and accountability. With the growth of social media and other digital platforms, more people are now able to participate in public discourse and share their experiences and perspectives. Citizen journalism provides a platform for marginalized voices to be heard. Traditional media outlets repeatedly neglect stories that are of interest to minority communities or those living in remote areas. Citizen journalists, on the other hand, can use their local knowledge and networks to report on events and issues that might otherwise be ignored. This can help give voice to those who have been historically marginalized and promote greater diversity in the public sphere.

It has also played a crucial role in exposing corruption and malpractice. In recent years, citizen journalists have used social media platforms to document instances of corruption and hold public officials accountable. For example, the *#MeToo* movement, which began in the United States and quickly spread to India, was driven in part by citizen journalists who shared their stories and experiences online. This led to a greater awareness of sexual harassment and assault in India and contributed to the passage of new laws and policies to address these issues.

Moreover, citizen journalism has also helped shape public opinion on crucial social and political issues in India. During the COVID-19 pandemic, citizen journalists provided critical information on the ground, including the availability of medical supplies and the status of healthcare facilities. This helped to fill gaps in official reporting and provided a more accurate picture of the situation. Citizen journalists also played a key role in reporting on the protests against the Citizenship Amendment Act (CAA) in 2019-20, which were largely ignored by mainstream media outlets. Their reporting helped raise awareness of the issues at stake and contributed to a broader public debate.

But, citizen journalism in India also faces some challenges. The lack of training and support can make it difficult for citizen journalists to ensure the accuracy and fairness of their reporting. Moreover, citizen journalists, over and over, face threats and harassment from those who disagree with their views, particularly on sensitive issues such as religion and caste. This can discourage some people from engaging in citizen journalism and limit the diversity of voices in the public sphere.

Citizen journalism has performed a critical duty in expanding the public sphere in India and promoting greater transparency and accountability. It has given voice to marginalized communities, exposed corruption and malpractice, and helped shape public opinion on important social and political issues. However, there is a need for greater support and training for citizen journalists, as well as efforts to address the challenges they face. By promoting greater diversity and inclusivity in the public sphere, citizen journalism can help strengthen democracy and promote social justice in India.

CHAPTER 5

CHALLENGES AND LIMITATIONS OF CITIZEN JOURNALISM

While citizen journalism has many positive aspects, it also has its drawbacks and potential negative effects. One of the most momentous negative aspects of citizen journalism is the lack of professionalism and training that generally comes with it. Professional journalists typically undergo rigorous training and adhere to a strict code of ethics. Citizen journalists, on the other hand, may lack this training and may not have the same level of experience in verifying sources, fact-checking, and understanding the broader context of a story. This can lead to inaccuracies, misinformation and even false information being disseminated.

Another potential negative aspect of citizen journalism is the lack of accountability. While traditional media outlets have a responsibility to report accurately and ethically, citizen journalists may not be held to the same standards. No regulating body oversees citizen journalism, and individuals may use the platform to push their own agendas or spread propaganda.

In addition, citizen journalism can lead to the spread of rumours and sensationalism. With the rise of social media, citizen journalists commonly use platforms such as Twitter and Facebook to report on events. While this can be beneficial in terms of providing real-time updates, it can also lead to the spread of unverified information and sensationalism. This can be especially damaging in situations where accurate and timely reporting is crucial, such as during natural disasters or political unrest.

Sometimes citizen journalism can risk harm to the individual journalists themselves. Citizen journalists may not have the same level of protection and security as professional journalists and may face retribution from those they report on. In some cases, citizen journalists have faced physical harm, legal repercussions, or harassment as a result of their reporting.

The democratization of news reporting that citizen journalism provides can lead to a lack of nuance and complexity. Traditional media outlets time and again have the resources to cover issues in-depth, whereas citizen journalists may not have the same level of access or resources. This can lead to a simplistic understanding of complex issues and events.

1. Challenges of Citizen Journalism

While citizen journalism has proven to be a powerful force in democratizing information and promoting diverse perspectives, it also faces several challenges. These challenges can impact the credibility and reliability of citizen-reported news. Here are some of the key challenges of citizen journalism:

i) Lack of Verification and Fact-Checking: Unlike professional journalists, citizen journalists may not always have the resources, training or time to thoroughly verify the accuracy of the information they report. This can lead to the dissemination of misinformation, rumours or unverified claims, which can harm public trust in citizen journalism as a reliable source of news.

ii) Bias and Subjectivity: Citizen journalists may bring their personal beliefs, opinions and biases into their reporting. While objectivity is an essential principle in journalism, citizen journalists may struggle to maintain neutrality, potentially leading to one-sided or ideologically driven coverage.

iii) Ethical Concerns: Citizen journalists continually lack a formal ethical framework and guidelines, which can lead to ethical dilemmas in their reporting. Issues such as invasion of privacy, the disclosure of sensitive information, and the protection of sources can arise when citizen journalists are not adequately trained in journalistic ethics.

iv) Limited Access and Resources: Unlike professional news organizations, citizen journalists may not have the same access to official sources, press conferences, or insider information. This limitation can result in incomplete or one-dimensional reporting, leaving important aspects of a story untold.

v) Safety Risks: Reporting on sensitive or dangerous topics can expose citizen journalists to safety risks. They may face threats, harassment or even physical harm while attempting to cover certain events, particularly in regions with political instability or conflict.

vi) Legal Issues: Citizen journalists may not be well-versed in media law and could unintentionally publish content that violates copyright laws, defamation laws or other legal regulations. This can lead to legal consequences for both the journalist and the platform hosting the content.

vii) Limited Audience Reach: While social media and online platforms have expanded the audience reach of citizen journalism, gaining a wide audience can still be challenging. Citizen journalists may struggle to compete with established media outlets in attracting a substantial and diverse readership.

viii) Misinterpretation and Sensationalism: Due to the speed at which information spreads on social media, citizen-reported news can be misinterpreted or sensationalized, leading to the spread of misinformation or exaggeration of events.

ix) Manipulation and Disinformation: Just as citizen journalism can be a force for truth, it can also be exploited for disinformation and propaganda. Bad actors may use social media platforms to spread false narratives or manipulate public opinion.

To address these challenges, citizen journalists need to receive training in journalistic principles, verification techniques, and ethical standards. Collaborating with professional journalists and news organizations can also help ensure the accuracy and credibility of citizen-reported news. As society continues to evolve, the role of citizen journalism will likely remain a dynamic and influential part of the media landscape, requiring ongoing adaptation and responsible practices to meet the highest standards of reporting.

2. Reliability and Accuracy

While citizen journalism has many benefits, one of the key challenges is ensuring reliability and accuracy.

Reliability and accuracy are essential in journalism because they determine the trustworthiness of the news source. In traditional journalism, reporters are trained to verify their sources and ensure that the information they report is accurate. However, citizen journalists do not always have the same level of training or experience. This can lead to flaws or even false information being shared.

One of the biggest challenges is the lack of editorial oversight. Professional news organizations have editors who review and fact-check stories before they are published. Citizen journalists, on the other hand, do not always have the benefit of this oversight. This can result in inaccuracies and errors that can be damaging to the credibility of citizen journalism as a whole.

Also, the speed and immediacy of social media can also contribute to the spread of false information. Citizen journalists may rush to report on breaking news without taking the time to verify their sources or the accuracy of the information. This can lead to the spread of rumours and misinformation that can be harmful.

3. Personal Bias and Prejudices in Citizen Journalism

Personal bias in journalism refers to an individual's inclination or prejudice towards a particular perspective or point of view that can influence their reporting. Journalists may have personal beliefs, values and experiences that shape their opinions and perspectives, which can influence the accuracy and objectivity of their reporting.

Personal bias can manifest in various ways, such as in the selection and interpretation of news sources, the framing of issues, and the choice of language used in reporting. It can also be influenced by external factors such as political affiliations, cultural norms and personal relationships. Furthermore, It can be problematic because it can lead to insufficient or unreliable reporting, as journalists may prioritize certain outlooks or ignore relevant information that contradicts their biases. It can also erode trust in journalism and lead to accusations of partisanship or agenda-driven reporting.

Promoting diversity and inclusivity is another way to address personal bias in citizen journalism. Ensuring that a range of perspectives and experiences are represented can help to reduce personal bias and increase the accuracy and objectivity of reporting.

One of the most common types of prejudices in journalism is political bias, where journalists may have preconceived notions about political parties, leaders or ideologies. This can result in unbalanced or unfair reporting, as journalists may ignore facts or standpoints that contradict their political biases.

Another form of prejudice in journalism is cultural bias, where journalists may hold preconceived opinions about certain cultures or ethnic groups, leading to stereotypical or discriminatory reporting. This can result in the under-representation or marginalization of certain communities and can perpetuate negative stereotypes and prejudices.

Gender bias is another form of prejudice in journalism, where journalists may hold preconceived opinions or attitudes towards individuals based on their gender. This can lead to under-representation or misrepresentation of certain gender identities or perpetuate gender stereotypes.

4. Hate Speech

Hate speech in journalism refers to the use of language that is intended to denigrate, intimidate, or harm individuals or groups based on their identity, such as race, ethnicity, gender, sexual orientation, religion or nationality. Hate speech can perpetuate stereotypes, fuel discrimination and violence, and have lasting psychological and social impacts on individuals and communities.

Hate speech in journalism can take various forms such as the use of derogatory language, perpetuating negative stereotypes or promoting harmful stereotypes. Hate speech can also be implicit like the selection and framing of news stories that reinforce negative attitudes towards certain groups.

It can have far-reaching consequences, including reinforcing systemic inequalities and social injustices. Moreover, it can also undermine the credibility and trustworthiness of journalists and media organizations, and harm their relationships with the communities they serve.

To address hate speech in journalism, it is essential to promote ethical and professional reporting practices that prioritize accuracy, fairness and impartiality. Journalists must be mindful of the language they use and the perspectives they present, avoiding any language or framing that could be perceived as hate speech. It is also vital to hold journalists and media organizations accountable for any instances of hate speech in their reporting. This can be achieved through public scrutiny, media criticismv and legal measures where appropriate.

5. Fake News

In recent years, the rise of citizen journalism has brought new challenges and opportunities to the world of media. While it has allowed for a greater diversity of voices and perspectives, it has also given rise to the phenomenon of fake news. Fake news in citizen journalism refers to the deliberate spread of false or misleading information by individuals who claim to be reporters or news sources.

One of the most significant impacts of fake news in citizen journalism is the erosion of trust in media. When false information is presented as fact, it can be difficult for readers to distinguish between what is real and what is not. This can lead to confusion, mistrust, and scepticism among the public, ultimately undermining the credibility of the entire media industry.

Fake news in citizen journalism can spread misinformation. Fake news can be used as a tool to manipulate public opinion, particularly during times of political or social unrest. It can also be used to spread hate speech or promote extremist views, further exacerbating existing social tensions. In this way, fake news can have a corrosive effect on democracy and human rights, by undermining the free flow of information and encouraging divisive and harmful narratives.

To combat fake news in citizen journalism, several measures can be taken. One of the most considerable measures is to promote media literacy and critical thinking skills among the public. This involves teaching people how to evaluate sources, identify bias and fact-check information. It also involves encouraging readers to question what they read and seek out multiple sources of information before forming an opinion.

Another measure is to promote ethical journalism practices among citizen journalists. This includes encouraging the use of reliable sources, fact-checking all information and avoiding the spread of sensational or unverified information. It also involves promoting transparency and accountability in reporting by disclosing potential conflicts of interest and correcting errors or inaccuracies when they occur.

6. Objectivity in Citizen Journalism

Objectivity is a fundamental principle of journalism that is often considered essential for ensuring the integrity and credibility of the profession. At its core, objectivity refers to the idea that journalists should strive to report the news impartially and neutrally, free from bias or personal opinion.

To strive for objectivity in citizen journalism, it is essential to adhere to ethical principles and standards, maintaining transparency about biases and conflicts of interest. Citizen journalists should also make efforts to present multiple approaches and provide context to their stories. It is important to strive for accuracy and fairness in reporting, regardless of personal beliefs or opinions.

It is worth noting that complete objectivity may not always be possible, especially in citizen journalism where reporters may be directly involved in the events they are covering or have personal connections to the people or issues they are reporting on. In such cases, it is crucial to disclose any potential biases or conflicts of interest to the audience.

Citizen journalism can also benefit from collaboration with professional journalists and news organizations. By working together, citizen journalists can learn from established journalistic practices and gain access to resources that can help them produce more accurate and reliable stories. Ultimately, while striving for objectivity is important, citizen journalism offers unique perceptions and insights that may not always align with traditional journalistic practices.

7. Quality Concerns

Quality in citizen journalism refers to the level of excellence, reliability and credibility of the stories and information produced by citizen journalists. The quality of citizen journalism is critical as it directly impacts the level of trust and credibility that readers and viewers have in the information presented.

To ensure quality in citizen journalism, citizen journalists should aim to produce accurate, reliable and well-researched stories. They should strive to verify information and sources, fact-check their stories and provide context and multiple perspectives to their reporting. Citizen journalists should also follow ethical principles, such as respecting the privacy and dignity of individuals involved in their stories and being transparent about potential conflicts of interest.

Another important aspect of quality in citizen journalism is the use of technology and tools to enhance the production of stories. Citizen journalists can use social media, video-sharing platforms, and other digital tools to reach a wider audience and provide engaging and interactive content. They can also use data visualization and other multimedia tools to enhance the quality and impact of their reporting.

8. Legal Ramifications

Citizen journalists may face legal challenges related to issues such as defamation, privacy, copyright infringement and national security concerns.

One of the most substantial legal issues faced by citizen journalists is defamation. Defamation occurs when a statement is made that harms a person's reputation or character. Citizen journalists must be careful to ensure that their reporting is factual and based on trustworthy sources. If a citizen journalist publishes false or misleading information that harms someone's reputation, they may be subject to a defamation lawsuit.

Another legal issue is privacy. Citizen journalists must be aware of the privacy rights of the individuals they are reporting on. If a citizen journalist publishes information that invades someone's privacy, they may be subject to legal action. For example, if a citizen journalist publishes photographs or videos of someone in a private setting without their consent, they may be violating that person's privacy rights.

Copyright infringement is another issue that citizen journalists may face. If a citizen journalist uses someone else's copyrighted material without permission, they may be subject to legal action. This can include using photographs, videos, or other content that is protected by copyright law.

National security concerns are also a potential legal issue for citizen journalists. If a citizen journalist publishes information that is classified or sensitive, they may be subject to legal action under national security laws. This can include publishing information that reveals confidential government operations or endangers national security.

In addition to these legal challenges, citizen journalists may also face challenges related to their status as non-professional journalists. Traditional journalists are usually granted certain legal protections such as shield laws that protect them from being forced to reveal their sources. However, these protections may not extend to citizen journalists who may not be considered professional journalists by the courts.

To mitigate these legal risks, citizen journalists must be careful to ensure that their reporting is accurate, based on reliable sources and does not violate the privacy or copyright rights of others. They may also want to seek legal advice to ensure that they are operating within the bounds of the law.

CHAPTER 6
CITIZEN JOURNALISM: LOOKING AHEAD

1. The Effects of Citizen Journalism on Traditional Journalism

Citizen journalism has had a significant impact on traditional journalism, both in terms of its practices and its influence on the industry as a whole. Some of the key effects of citizen journalism on traditional journalism include:

i) Increased competition: Citizen Journalism has opened up the media landscape to a wider range of voices and perspectives, creating more competition for traditional news organizations. With more people able to publish and share news and information online, traditional news organizations must work harder to differentiate themselves and maintain their relevance. This has led to a greater focus on quality journalism and innovative storytelling techniques.

ii) Greater diversity of voices: Citizen Journalism has launched new paradigms and voices into the media realm, providing a more diverse range of viewpoints on news and events. This has helped address the under-representation of marginalized groups in traditional journalism and has increased the quality and accuracy of reporting. By including more heterogeneous voices, traditional journalism can better reflect the communities it serves.

iii) A shift in power dynamics: Citizen Journalism has challenged the traditional power dynamics in journalism, where a small group of professionals were responsible for determining what news was important and how it was reported. With citizen journalists able to publish their own stories and opinions, traditional journalists must now engage with and respond to a wider range of voices. This has led to a stronger democratic and inclusive media landscape.

iv) A new focus on immediacy and speed: Citizen Journalism has emphasized the importance of speed and immediacy in reporting, with citizen journalists frequently breaking news before traditional news organizations. This has put pressure on traditional journalists to report news more quickly and has led to an increased focus on breaking news and real-time reporting. However, this focus on speed can also lead to inaccuracies and misinformation, which must be carefully managed.

v) A need for greater accuracy and fact-checking: While citizen journalism has brought novel voices and perspectives to the media landscape, it has also raised concerns about the accuracy and reliability of reporting. Traditional journalists must now work harder to check the facts and verify information from citizen journalists and must take greater care to ensure that their reporting is precise and impartial. This has led to a greater focus on fact-checking and accountability in journalism.

The rise of citizen journalism has transformed the media environment, creating new opportunities and challenges for traditional journalists and news organizations. While it has increased competition and challenged traditional power dynamics, it has also brought new voices and perspectives to the forefront of journalism, creating a more diverse and democratic media domain.

2. Citizen Journalism and the Digital Age

The digital age has transformed the way people consume and produce news. With the rise of social media and other digital platforms, citizen journalism has emerged as a powerful tool for individuals to share information and report on events that traditional news organizations may not cover. Citizen journalism has the potential to democratize the news and increase the diversity of voices in the public discourse.

Citizen journalism in the digital age has the potential to increase access to information and promote transparency. With the proliferation of digital devices, individuals can capture and share news in real time, providing a distinct outlook on events that may not be covered by traditional news organizations. This can include grassroots movements, protests and other events that may be overlooked by mainstream media. Citizen journalists can also serve as a check on the power of traditional media organizations, providing a critical framework for their reporting and potentially exposing partialities or inaccuracies.

Citizen journalism in the digital age also presents challenges related to accuracy and reliability. With the abundance of information available online, it can be difficult for individuals to discern what is true and what is not. Citizen journalists may also lack the training and resources of professional journalists, leading to potential inaccuracies or misreporting.

In addition, citizen journalism in the digital age can raise ethical considerations related to privacy and consent. Citizen journalists must be aware of the privacy rights of the individuals they are reporting on and ensure that they have obtained proper consent for any photographs or videos they capture. They must also be careful not to contribute to the spread of false information or hate speech.

The digital age has also presented new legal challenges for citizen journalists. As previously mentioned, citizen journalists may face legal challenges related to defamation, privacy, copyright infringement and national security concerns. Moreover, they may also face challenges related to access as some events or locations may be restricted to traditional journalists.

Despite these challenges, citizen journalism in the digital age has the potential to promote transparency and accountability in the news. By providing a diversity of perspectives and reporting on events that may be overlooked by traditional media, citizen journalists can contribute to a more informed public discourse.

3. New Trends in Citizen Journalism.

Citizen journalists have become catalysts for change, amplifying diverse voices, challenging narratives and fostering informed and engaged societies. Empowering individuals to report, analyze, and share news and information, citizen journalism has become a force to be reckoned with in the media sphere. The emerging trends in citizen journalism highlight how they contribute to the democratization of information, the amplification of multifaceted voices, and the potential for positive societal impact. The new trends in citizen journalism underscore the transformative power of technology and the expanding role of individuals in shaping the news landscape. As these trends continue to evolve, citizen journalism will undoubtedly play a pivotal role in shaping the future of media.

The different news trends in Citizen Journalism are i) Live reporting ii) Collaborative journalism, iii) Mobile journalism, iv) Data journalism, v) Crowdfunding and vi) Virtual reality.

4. Live Reporting

Live streaming in citizen journalism refers to the practice of broadcasting events, incidents, or news stories in real time using live streaming platforms such as Facebook Live, YouTube Live, Instagram Live, Periscope or other similar services. It allows citizen journalists to capture and share live video footage with their audience as events unfold.

It is one of the most influential trends in citizen journalism. Citizen journalists armed with smartphones can now provide instant coverage of breaking news, protests, and events as they unfold. Live streaming not only allows individuals to share authentic, unfiltered perspectives but also creates a sense of immediacy and engagement for viewers around the world.

Live streaming enables citizen journalists to provide instant coverage of breaking news, protests, rallies, natural disasters and other significant events. They can report from the scene and share information timely, offering viewers a front-row seat to unfolding events. They provide an unfiltered, raw perspective of events. Unlike traditional news coverage, which is regularly edited and curated, live streaming offers a direct and unvarnished view of what is happening on the ground. This authenticity helps build trust and credibility with the audience.

It allows for instantaneous interaction between citizen journalists and their audience. Viewers can comment, ask questions and engage in discussions during the broadcast, creating a more dynamic and participatory experience. This immediate feedback loop enhances engagement and fosters a sense of community around the coverage. Live streaming transcends geographical boundaries and enables citizen journalists to reach a global audience. Viewers from different parts of the world can tune in and get firsthand information about events in real time, regardless of their physical location.

Live streaming requires minimal equipment, primarily a smartphone with a camera and an internet connection. It eliminates the need for elaborate production setups, making it a cost-effective method of reporting for citizen journalists. This accessibility ensures that anyone with a smartphone can become a live reporter, democratizing the field of journalism. They can be saved and archived, serving as valuable records of events. They can be referred to in the future for research, verification, or documentation purposes. This feature helps preserve and maintain a historical record of events as witnessed by citizen journalists.

Live streaming has become an integral part of citizen journalism, empowering individuals to report news and share information at the moment. By leveraging the immediacy, authenticity, interactivity and global reach of live-streaming platforms, citizen journalists contribute to a more diverse, inclusive and decentralized news landscape.

5. Collaborative Journalism

Collaborative journalism, also known as cooperative journalism, is a form of journalism where reporters, media outlets, and/or citizen journalists work together to investigate and report on a specific story or issue. This approach to journalism has gained popularity in recent years due to its ability to provide in-depth coverage of complex issues, bring together diverse perspectives, and hold those in power accountable.

Collaborative journalism can take many forms, from joint investigations to the sharing of resources and expertise. It can involve journalists from different outlets, including print, digital and broadcast, working together to investigate a story. Alternatively, it can involve journalists and citizens collaborating to uncover and document a particular issue or event.

It has become more prevalent in the digital age, as journalists and media outlets can work together from various parts of the world to investigate and record stories that may have otherwise gone unnoticed. It can also involve the use of social media and online platforms to connect with and engage communities.

One of the benefits of collaborative journalism is the ability to bring together differing outlooks and expertise. This can lead to more nuanced and comprehensive reporting as well as greater public engagement with the issue being covered. Collaborative journalism can also provide a platform for voices that may have been marginalized in traditional media. It allows for the pooling of resources and expertise and can lead to impactful reporting that holds those in power accountable. As media landscapes continue to evolve, collaborative journalism is likely to play an increasingly important role in shaping the future of journalism.

6. Mobile journalism

Mobile journalism, also known as MoJo, refers to the practice of using mobile devices, such as smartphones or tablets, to capture and produce news content. With the rise of smartphones and mobile technology, mobile journalism has become an increasingly popular and important tool for journalists and media organizations.

One of the prime benefits of mobile journalism is its accessibility. With just a smartphone and a few basic tools, anyone can capture and share news content from virtually anywhere. This has made it possible for journalists and citizen journalists alike to report on events and stories that might otherwise go unreported.

Mobile journalism has also helped break down traditional barriers to entry in the field of journalism. With the cost of professional-grade cameras and other equipment prohibitively high for many aspiring journalists, mobile technology has made it possible for anyone with a smartphone to start reporting and producing content.

Mobile journalism has made it easier for citizen journalists to cover breaking news stories from the field, without the need for expensive equipment or extensive training. With a smartphone and an internet connection, citizen journalists can capture video, audio, and photos of events as they unfold, and share them on social media platforms like Twitter, Facebook and Instagram. This has enabled them to become active participants in the news cycle and has helped to break down the barriers between professional journalists and ordinary citizens.

It has also given citizen journalists the ability to cover stories that may not have received mainstream media coverage. By capturing and sharing footage of events that may have otherwise gone unnoticed, citizen journalists have helped shine a light on important issues that may have been ignored by traditional media outlets.

7. Data Journalism

Data journalism is a form of journalism that involves using data analysis and visualization techniques to report news stories. It involves the collection, analysis, and presentation of data to uncover important trends, patterns and insights that might otherwise be missed by traditional journalistic methods.

In data journalism, journalists use various tools and techniques to gather and analyze data. They may use statistical software or programming languages such as R or Python to analyze large data sets, or they may use data visualization tools such as Tableau or D3.js to create interactive charts and graphs that help visualize complex data.

The rise of data journalism has been driven in part by the explosion of digital data in recent years. With more and more information being created and stored online, journalists have access to an unprecedented amount of data that can be used to inform their reporting. In addition, the increasing availability of open data sets and government data portals has made it easier for journalists to access and analyze data.

One of the finest advantages of data journalism is that it allows journalists to uncover important stories and insights that might otherwise be missed. By analyzing data, journalists can identify patterns and trends that are not immediately apparent and can use this information to develop more in-depth and insightful reporting.

Another merit is that it allows journalists to present information more engagingly and interactively. By using data visualization tools, journalists can create interactive charts and graphs that allow readers to explore data sets and draw their own conclusions. This can help to increase engagement with readers and can help to make complex information more accessible.

Data journalism has emerged as an unavoidable tool for journalists in the digital age. By using data analysis and visualization techniques, journalists can unveil important stories and insights and can present information participatory. As the amount of data available to journalists continues to grow, data journalism is likely to become an increasingly important part of the journalistic toolkit.

Data journalism and citizen journalism can work together to create a more comprehensive understanding of events and issues. Data journalism provides citizen journalists with access to factual information that can be used to support their reporting.

One example of how data journalism and citizen journalism can work together is in the coverage of environmental issues. Data journalists can use satellite imagery and other scientific data to investigate pollution levels, deforestation rates and other environmental concerns. Citizen journalists can then report on the local impact of these issues and share stories about how they affect their communities.

8. Crowdfunding

Crowdfunding in journalism is a method of financing where individuals contribute small amounts of money to support the creation and distribution of journalistic content. It allows journalists to bypass traditional sources of funding, such as advertising revenue or institutional grants, and instead rely on a large group of individual donors to finance their work.

Crowdfunding can take many forms, from donation-based models where contributors receive no tangible benefit beyond the satisfaction of supporting a worthy cause, to reward-based models where contributors receive perks or rewards in exchange for their contributions. In journalism, reward-based crowdfunding might involve offering early access to articles, exclusive interviews with sources, or other perks that are relevant to the content being produced.

One of the major advancements of crowdfunding in journalism is that it allows journalists to maintain editorial independence and pursue stories that might not be attractive to traditional funders. By relying on a large group of individual donors, journalists can avoid being beholden to any particular interest group or institution, and can instead focus on producing high-quality, impactful journalism. It has become a growingly popular method of financing journalism in recent years, as traditional funding sources have become more difficult to access and as the public has become more interested in supporting independent journalism.

The rise of crowdfunding has been driven in part by the changing media landscape. With the decline of traditional media organizations and the rise of digital media, many journalists have found themselves without access to the resources or funding that they need to produce high-quality journalism. Crowdfunding has emerged as a way for these journalists to finance their reporting and investigations, generally by appealing directly to their audience for support.

Citizen journalism has emerged as a powerful complement to crowdfunding, as it provides a means for individuals to produce and distribute news and information without the need for institutional support. Through social media and other digital platforms, citizen journalists can report on local events and issues, commonly providing exceptional standpoint that is not available through traditional media outlets.

Through crowdfunding, journalists can raise funds to cover their expenses, such as travel, equipment and research. They can also use the funds to pay themselves for their work, as many journalists operate as freelancers or volunteers. By raising funds in this way, journalists can maintain their independence and pursue stories that might not be attractive to traditional funders.

9. Virtual Reality

Virtual reality (VR) has emerged as a powerful tool for immersive storytelling and is increasingly being used in journalism to bring audiences closer to the stories that they are reading. VR allows journalists to create interactive and immersive experiences that can transport viewers to the heart of a story, giving them a sense of what it is like to be there in person.

The most important advantage of VR in journalism is its ability to provide a more visceral and emotional connection between the viewer and the story. By creating a fully immersive environment, VR can help break down the barrier between the viewer and the story, making it easier for them to engage with the material and understand its implications.

VR can be particularly effective in telling stories that are difficult to convey through traditional media, such as those involving conflict, disaster or other high-stress situations. By creating a virtual environment that simulates the sights and sounds of the event, VR can help viewers to better understand the impact of these events on the people who are affected by them.

Virtual Reality provides a more engaging and interactive experience for the viewer. By allowing viewers to explore a virtual environment, interact with objects, and engage with other characters, VR can create a more immersive and engaging experience that is more akin to a video game than a traditional news article.

The combination of VR and citizen journalism has the potential to create a powerful new form of storytelling that is both immersive and democratic. By using VR to create immersive environments that simulate the sights and sounds of a story, citizen journalists can provide a more visceral and emotional connection to their reporting, making it easier for viewers to engage with the material and understand its implications.

Using VR in citizen journalism provides a more accurate and comprehensive representation of a story. By creating a virtual environment that simulates the sights and sounds of an event, citizen journalists can provide a more nuanced and detailed view of the story, helping viewers to better understand the impact of the event on the people who are affected by it.

10. Media Freedom in the Age of Citizen Journalism

Media freedom has always been a vital component of any democracy, allowing for the free exchange of ideas and information. However, in the age of citizen journalism, media freedom has taken on new dimensions, with citizens empowered to report on events and issues that traditional media may not cover. While citizen journalism has the potential to expand media freedom, it also presents new challenges and ethical considerations that must be addressed.

One of the major privileges of citizen journalism in the age of media freedom is the ability to boost the diversity of voices and perspectives in the public discourse. Traditional media outlets usually have their own biases and perspectives that can limit the range of views presented to the public. Citizen journalism, on the other hand, allows for a wider range of views and perspectives to be presented, leading to a more informed public discourse.

Citizen journalism in the age of media freedom can also promote transparency and accountability in the news. Citizen journalists are repeatedly able to narrate events and issues that may be overlooked by traditional media, providing critical viewpoints and insights that can hold those in power accountable.

The rise of citizen journalism in the age of media freedom has also led to concerns around privacy and consent. Citizen journalists must be aware of the privacy rights of the individuals they are detailing and ensure that they have obtained proper consent for any photographs or videos they capture. They must also be careful not to contribute to the spread of false information or hate speech.

Citizen journalists in the age of media freedom may also face legal challenges related to defamation, privacy, copyright infringement and national security concerns. As such, it is important for citizen journalists to understand their legal rights and obligations and to ensure that their reporting is based on reliable sources and adheres to ethical and legal standards.

To address these challenges and ensure media freedom in the age of citizen journalism, governments need to protect and promote the rights of citizens to freely express their opinions and ideas. This can include protecting the anonymity of citizen journalists, providing legal protections for their reporting, and supporting initiatives that promote media literacy and critical thinking.

Moreover, traditional media outlets can also take a role in promoting media freedom in the age of citizen journalism. By partnering with citizen journalists and providing them with training and resources, traditional media outlets can help ensure the accuracy and reliability of citizen journalism. They can also promote a culture of ethical and responsible reporting, which can supporet to counteract the potential biases and inaccuracies that can arise in citizen journalism.

11. Citizen Journalism and Youth

In today's digital age, where information flows rapidly and media landscapes evolve, citizen journalism has emerged as a powerful tool for youth to reclaim their voices and actively participate in shaping public discourse. As young individuals navigate a world of complex challenges and unique angles, citizen journalism provides them with an avenue to express their thoughts, raise awareness about critical issues and influence societal change.

i) Amplifying Youth Voices: Citizen journalism offers a platform for young people to amplify their voices and share their experiences, concerns and aspirations. Traditional media, over and over, fails to capture the multifaceted perspectives of youth, but citizen journalism empowers them to become active participants in the news-making process. By leveraging social media, blogs and other digital platforms, youth citizen journalists can reach broader audiences, ensuring that their voices are heard and their stories are shared.

ii) Fostering Engagement and Empowerment: Engaging in citizen journalism empowers young individuals to take ownership of the issues they care about and become agents of change. By reporting on local events, social issues, or community initiatives, youth citizen journalists inspire others to get involved, creating a ripple effect of engagement. Through their contributions, young people develop a sense of agency, realizing that they can make a difference and influence public opinion and policy.

iii) Developing Critical Thinking Skills: Citizen journalism encourages youth to analyze and evaluate information critically. As citizen journalists, they must fact-check, verify sources and present balanced viewpoints. This process cultivates their critical thinking skills, teaching them to question narratives, challenge assumptions, and develop a discerning eye for media content. By becoming media-savvy, young citizen journalists can better navigate the information landscape, separating fact from fiction and combating misinformation.

iv) Addressing Underreported Youth Issues: Mainstream media many times overlooks or underreports issues that directly affect youth. Citizen journalism provides an opportunity for young people to shed light on these topics, ranging from mental health challenges to educational disparities, environmental activism, or social justice concerns. By reporting on these underrepresented issues, youth citizen journalists can raise awareness, spark conversations and advocate for positive change in their communities.

v) Bridging the Generation Gap: Citizen journalism offers a rare opportunity for intergenerational dialogue and understanding. As young people contribute their perspectives, experiences, and ideas, they bridge the gap between generations, fostering mutual respect and empathy. Citizen journalism serves as a catalyst for constructive conversations, breaking down stereotypes and misconceptions, and building bridges of understanding and collaboration between youth and adults.

vi) Nurturing Media Literacy: Engaging in citizen journalism helps youth develop media literacy skills. By actively participating in the production and dissemination of news, they gain a sources, and become discerning media consumers who can deeper understanding of media processes, biases and the importance of ethical reporting. This knowledge equips them to critically consume media content, distinguish between reliable and unreliable differentiate between wide-ranging viewpoints.

vii) Inspiring Social Activism: Youth citizen journalists often become a trigger for social activism, inspiring others to take action and driving positive change. By shedding light on injustices, advocating for marginalized communities, and promoting social causes, they mobilize their peers and wider audiences. Through citizen journalism, young individuals realize their collective power and become forces for social justice equity and inclusivity.

Citizen journalism empowers youth to reclaim their voices, actively engage in societal issues and shape public discourse. By providing platforms for expression, fostering critical thinking skills and amplifying underrepresented perspectives, citizen journalism serves as a stimulus for positive change. As young individuals become citizen journalists.

12. Jay Rosen's Views on Citizen Journalism

Jay Rosen is a prominent media critic and journalism professor at New York University who has been a strong advocate for citizen journalism. Rosen has argued that traditional journalism has been too focused on the idea of objectivity and has failed to engage with its audience in a meaningful way. He believes that citizen journalism has the potential to be a transformative force in the news media, allowing for a more diverse range of perspectives and voices to be heard.

Rosen has identified several key benefits of citizen journalism, including its ability to democratize the news media, provide a platform for marginalized voices and foster a more engaged and informed public. He has also argued that citizen journalism can help to fill gaps in traditional news coverage, particularly in areas where there may be limited access to mainstream media.

One of Rosen's main arguments for citizen journalism is that it can help popularise the news media. Traditional news organizations are frequently controlled by a small group of gatekeepers who determine what news is important and how it should be covered. This can result in a narrow range of standpoints being represented in the news, and significant stories being overlooked or ignored. By contrast, citizen journalists are generally members of the communities they report on, and are more likely to have a deeper understanding of local issues and concerns. This can result in a more diverse range of perspectives being represented in the news, and a more inclusive and engaged news media overall.

Rosen has also argued that citizen journalism can provide a platform for marginalized voices. Traditional news organizations have historically been dominated by white, male, and middle-class outlooks, and have commonly failed to represent the experiences and perceptions of women, people of colour and other marginalized groups. Citizen journalists, on the other hand, can bring their own unique attitudes and insights to the news and can help amplify the voices of those who have been historically excluded from the news media.

Another primary asset of citizen journalism, according to Rosen, is that it can help foster a more engaged and informed public. Traditional news organizations have long struggled with declining audiences and a lack of trust among the public. By contrast, citizen journalism can create a more participatory and collaborative relationship between journalists and their audiences and can help to build trust and credibility in the news media. By engaging with their audiences and involving them in the news-gathering process, citizen journalists can help create a more informed and engaged public, which can in turn lead to greater civic participation and a more vibrant democracy.

Rosen has also acknowledged the challenges and risks associated with citizen journalism. One of the biggest risks is the potential for false or misleading information to be spread, particularly on social media. Citizen journalists may not have the same level of training or experience as professional journalists, and may not be held to the same standards of accuracy and impartiality. As a result, it's important for citizen journalists to follow proper journalistic standards and ethics, and for news organizations to provide training and support for citizen journalists to help them navigate these challenges.

Rosen's advocacy for citizen journalism has helped to raise awareness about the potential of this type of reporting and its role in shaping the future of the news media. By promoting greater collaboration and engagement between journalists and their audiences, Rosen has facilitated to fostering of a more open and participatory culture in the news media, paving the way for a more diverse and inclusive future for journalism.

13. Hyperlocal Journalism

Hyperlocal journalism refers to news coverage that focuses on a specific geographic area, such as a neighbourhood, community, or town. The rise of digital media has enabled hyperlocal journalism to flourish, with many news outlets and independent journalists using online platforms to provide in-depth coverage of local events and issues.

Hyperlocal journalism is significant because it helps create a sense of community by providing news and information that is relevant to local residents. It offers a space for local voices to be heard and for important issues to be discussed. Unlike traditional news outlets, which cover national or international news, hyperlocal journalism focuses on topics that directly impact the lives of local residents. This can include reporting on local government decisions, events and activities, and community issues such as crime, education, and infrastructure.

Hyperlocal journalism can help bridge the gap between residents and local government. By reporting on local government decisions and policies, hyperlocal journalists can hold local officials accountable and help to ensure that the public is informed about decisions that impact their lives. This can contribute to greater transparency and accountability in local government, which is essential for a functioning democracy.

It can also provide a platform for underrepresented communities to be heard. Traditional news outlets often overlook issues that are of importance to specific communities, such as those based on race, ethnicity, or socioeconomic status. Hyper-local journalists can provide a platform for these communities to share their stories and experiences and raise awareness about important issues. This can help promote greater understanding and empathy between different communities and promote social justice.

But, hyperlocal journalism also faces some complications. One of the key hurdles is financial sustainability, as hyperlocal news outlets continually struggle to generate sufficient revenue to support their operations. Many hyperlocal journalists work independently, without the resources and support of larger news organizations. This can make it difficult to cover breaking news events or to invest in investigative journalism.

Another struggle is ensuring the accuracy and quality of reporting. With the rise of social media, it can be difficult to separate fact from fiction, and hyper-local journalists must be diligent in fact-checking and verifying information. This requires significant resources and training, which can be difficult to obtain for independent journalists.

Hyperlocal journalism is a vital component of modern journalism. It provides an essential service by informing local residents about news and events that directly impact their lives. It can also provide a platform for underrepresented communities to be heard and to raise awareness about important issues.

14. The Future of Citizen Journalism

Citizen journalism has come a long way in the last few decades, from a niche movement of amateur reporters to a force that has transformed the media landscape. With the rise of social media and other online platforms, anyone with a smartphone or a laptop can report on events, share their opinions and influence public opinion.

The future of citizen journalism looks promising, with many opportunities for growth and innovation. Here are some key trends that are likely to shape the future of citizen journalism.

i) Increased diversity and inclusivity: Citizen Journalism has the potential to promote greater diversity and inclusivity in media representation. By giving voice to those who have been traditionally marginalized, citizen journalism can provide a more accurate and representative portrayal of society. As more people from diverse backgrounds become involved in citizen journalism, we can expect to see a wider range of perspectives and stories being shared.

ii) More collaboration with traditional media: While citizen journalism has challenged the traditional media, there are also opportunities for collaboration between the two. Many professional journalists are now incorporating citizen journalism into their reporting, using social media to gather information, and featuring citizen journalists' stories on their platforms. This collaboration can benefit both parties, with citizen journalists gaining access to a wider audience, and professional journalists benefiting from the distinct attitude and insights of citizen journalists.

iii) Greater emphasis on verification and fact-checking: As citizen journalism continues to grow, there is a growing need for better verification and fact-checking. With so much information being shared online, it can be difficult to separate fact from fiction. In the future, we can expect to see more tools and technologies being developed to help citizen journalists verify their sources and ensure the accuracy of their reporting.

iv) New technologies and platforms: New technologies and platforms are likely to continue to shape the future of citizen journalism. Advances in virtual reality and augmented reality, for example, could enable citizen journalists to provide immersive experiences that bring their stories to life. New platforms and apps may also emerge, providing new ways for citizen journalists to share their stories and connect with audiences.

v) Greater emphasis on ethical standards: As citizen journalism becomes more mainstream, there will be increasing pressure to establish ethical standards and guidelines. This will be important to ensure that citizen journalists adhere to principles such as accuracy, fairness, and impartiality. Professional organizations may emerge to provide guidance and support to citizen journalists, helping to promote high standards of journalism.

vi) Increased focus on local news and community journalism: As traditional media outlets continue to struggle financially, there is a growing need for local news and community journalism. Citizen journalists are well-positioned to provide coverage of local events and issues, giving voice to local communities and filling a gap in the media landscape. In the future, we can expect to see more citizen journalists focusing on hyperlocal news and community reporting.

The future of citizen journalism looks bright. With new technologies and platforms, greater emphasis on verification and ethical standards, and increasing collaboration with traditional media, citizen journalism is poised to become an even more influential force in the media landscape. As more people become involved in citizen journalism, we can expect to see a more diverse, inclusive, and accurate portrayal of society, with citizen journalists playing a key role in shaping public opinion and promoting accountability and transparency.

15. Top Websites for Citizen Journalism

1) Global Voices: Global Voices is a well-known website and community that focuses on citizen journalism and amplifying voices from around the world. It was founded in 2005 by Ethan Zuckerman and Rebecca MacKinnon. The platform serves as a space for individuals, activists, and journalists to share stories and perspectives from their regions, often covering topics and events that might not receive mainstream media attention. Global Voices collaborates with a network of writers, translators, and volunteers from various countries and linguistic backgrounds. This allows them to provide content in multiple languages and offer insights from a wide range of perspectives.

Global Voices promotes citizen journalism, where everyday people contribute stories, photos, and videos about events and issues in their communities. This approach helps provide a more grassroots and authentic view of global events. The website covers a wide range of topics, including politics, human rights, culture, technology, and more. This diversity of coverage helps readers gain insights into various aspects of different societies.

Since the contributors come from different parts of the world, many articles are translated into multiple languages, making the content accessible to a global audience. Beyond reporting news and stories, Global Voices also engages in advocacy and activism efforts related to freedom of expression, digital rights, and other issues affecting online communities.

2) OhmyNews: OhmyNews is a South Korean online news website that gained international recognition for its pioneering approach to citizen journalism. It was founded by Oh Yeon-ho in 2000. The platform's unique model allowed ordinary citizens to contribute articles and become reporters, blurring the lines between traditional journalism and citizen-generated content.

It was one of the earliest platforms to fully embrace the concept of citizen journalism. It allowed anyone to submit news articles, opinion pieces, and reports, democratizing the process of news creation. Instead of relying solely on professional journalists, OhmyNews encouraged citizen participation in reporting. This model aimed to provide diverse perspectives and cover stories that might not receive attention from traditional media outlets.

OhmyNews aimed to promote democratic engagement by giving a voice to people from all walks of life. It helped bridge the gap between the public and decision-makers through citizen-generated content. Operating primarily online, OhmyNews utilized the internet's reach to distribute news and information quickly and efficiently.

3) GroundUp: GroundUp is a South African news organization known for its focus on citizen journalism and its commitment to covering stories that often go unreported by mainstream media. GroundUp operates as a platform for citizen journalism, allowing community members, activists, and ordinary citizens to contribute stories and reports about issues affecting their communities.

The platform is particularly dedicated to reporting on social justice issues, human rights, and matters of public interest. It often highlights stories that might be overlooked by traditional media outlets. GroundUp collaborates with various organizations, journalists, and writers to create a network of contributors. This approach enables a diverse range of perspectives and voices to be heard.

4) Newzulu: Newzulu is a platform that enabled citizen journalists and eyewitnesses to submit photos, videos, and reports of news events happening around the world. It aimed to provide a platform for individuals to share firsthand accounts of news stories, often from their local perspectives. The platform focused on user-generated content, which could include photos, videos, and written reports. This content was often submitted by individuals who were present at the scene of an event as it unfolded.

5) Citizen Matters: Citizen Matters is an Indian media organization that focuses on hyperlocal news and citizen journalism. It provides news, analysis, and features related to urban living and governance, with an emphasis on community-level reporting. The organization aims to empower citizens by providing them with relevant and actionable information about their localities.

While Citizen Matters has a team of professional journalists, it also encourages citizens to contribute their stories, insights, and observations about their communities. This approach helps create a collaborative and community-driven news platform. The platform covers a wide range of topics relevant to urban residents, including governance, infrastructure, education, health, environment, and more.

16. The Dhruv Rathee Effect: Transforming Public Discourse Through Citizen Journalism

In the modern age of media, the landscape of journalism has undergone a seismic shift, largely influenced by the rise of digital platforms and the democratization of information dissemination. Among the many voices contributing to this transformation, Dhruv Rathee has emerged as a prominent figure, exemplifying the role of a citizen journalist. Through his incisive analysis, data-driven approach, and commitment to questioning authority, Rathee has redefined how ordinary individuals can participate in shaping public discourse.

Dhruv Rathee, a young YouTuber and activist, began his journey into citizen journalism with a mission to educate the masses on pressing socio-political and environmental issues. Starting as a content creator focusing on environmental awareness, Rathee soon expanded his scope to include political commentary, policy analysis, and social issues. His videos often challenge government policies and mainstream media narratives, making him a voice of dissent in a media environment that many perceive as increasingly polarized.

One of Rathee's defining traits is his commitment to presenting facts and statistics. He meticulously researches his topics, ensuring that his content is not only engaging but also credible. This approach has garnered him a significant following, particularly among the youth, who resonate with his clear, concise, and informative style.

Rathee's work as a citizen journalist has had a profound impact on the public sphere in India. By leveraging digital platforms, he has created a space where alternative viewpoints can flourish. Rathee consistently sheds light on issues often overlooked by mainstream media, such as environmental degradation, corruption, and social justice. For instance, his videos on climate change and pollution provide detailed explanations and actionable solutions, encouraging viewers to engage with these pressing issues. Rathee is unafraid to question authority and hold those in power accountable. His critiques of government policies are often backed by thorough research, making his arguments difficult to dismiss. This has positioned him as a credible counter-narrative to mainstream media, which is sometimes criticized for being overly sympathetic to the establishment. His videos inspire civic participation by encouraging his audience to think critically about governance, policies, and societal issues. By highlighting the importance of accountability and transparency, he fosters a sense of responsibility among his viewers to actively engage in democratic processes.

Despite his contributions, Rathee's work as a citizen journalist is not without controversy. Critics accuse him of political bias, alleging that his content disproportionately targets specific political parties or ideologies. His outspoken stance has made him a target of online harassment and trolling, reflecting the challenges faced by citizen journalists in a polarized digital environment. The lack of formal journalistic training can be a double-edged sword. While Rathee's independence allows for unfiltered commentary, it also leaves him vulnerable to accusations of partisanship or incomplete analysis. These criticisms highlight the broader challenges of citizen journalism, where the absence of editorial oversight can sometimes compromise credibility.

Rathee's rise as a citizen journalist must be understood within the broader context of media evolution in India. The increasing corporatization of traditional media and allegations of bias have created a demand for alternative sources of information. Citizen journalists like Rathee fill this void, offering diverse perspectives that challenge the status quo.

The advent of social media has empowered individuals to bypass traditional gatekeepers of information. Platforms like YouTube, Twitter, and Instagram have enabled citizen journalists to reach global audiences, democratizing the flow of information.

Rathee's success is a testament to the potential of these platforms to amplify independent voices and reshape public discourse.